Microsoft System Center 2016 Orchestrator Cookbook

Second Edition

Simplify the automation of your administrative tasks

Michael Seidl
Andreas Baumgarten
Steve Beaumont
Samuel Erskine

BIRMINGHAM - MUMBAI

Microsoft System Center 2016 Orchestrator Cookbook

Second Edition

First published: August 2013

Second edition: July 2017

Production reference: 1240717

Published by Packt Publishing Ltd.
Livery Place
35 Livery Street
Birmingham
B3 2PB, UK.

ISBN 978-1-78646-046-2

www.packtpub.com

Credits

Authors
Michael Seidl
Andreas Baumgarten
Steve Beaumont
Samuel Erskine

Reviewer
Rafael Delgado

Commissioning Editor
Vijin Boricha

Acquisition Editor
Meeta Rajani

Content Development Editor
Abhishek Jadhav

Technical Editor
Mohd Riyan Khan

Copy Editors
Juliana Nair
Yesha Gangani

Project Coordinator
Judie Jose

Proofreader
Safis Editing

Indexer
Aishwarya Gangawane

Graphics
Kirk D'Penha

Production Coordinator
Aparna Bhagat

About the Authors

Michael Seidl is a senior consultant and team leader in service management and automation, working for Base-IT, a Gold Partner in Systems Management, located in Austria. He is a two-time System Center Cloud and Datacenter Management MVP and a well-certified Microsoft Engineer with MCSA and MCSE.

His experience as an IT consultant has been growing since 2001 and is mainly focused on SCDPM, SCO, SCSM, and PowerShell. Working with some of the biggest companies in Austria gives him the opportunity to work on great projects with complex requirements. Michael is focused on transforming IT departments through service management, systems management, cloud technologies, and automation.

Michael regularly shares his experience on the TechNet Forum. You can follow him on Twitter at @TechguyAt. His Facebook page is TechguyAT.

> *I would like to thank my girlfriend, Jasmine, in being very sympathetic with me on spending much time on writing this book, although since she is pregnant with our first child and would have needed some more of my time.*
>
> *Also, thanks to Stephan Burger on trying to be a reviewer.*

Andreas Baumgarten is a Microsoft MVP and works as an IT Architect with the German IT service provider H&D International Group. He has been working as an IT professional for more than 20 years. Microsoft technologies have always accompanied him, and he can also look back on more than 14 years' experience as a Microsoft Certified Trainer.

Since 2008, he has been responsible for the field of Microsoft System Center technology consulting and ever since has taken part in Microsoft System Center Service Manager (2010, 2012, 2012 R2 and 2016); additionally, he has participated in the Microsoft System Center Technology Adoption Program with H&D since many years.

With his deep inside-technology know-how and his broad experience across the Microsoft System Center product family and IT management, he now designs and develops private and hybrid cloud solutions for customers all over Germany and Europe.

In July 2017, he was awarded the Microsoft Most Valuable Professional (MVP) title for System Center Cloud and Datacenter Management for the sixth year in a row.

Steve Beaumont has worked for more years than he cares to admit within IT, starting with desktop support. He is now the Product Development Director of PowerONPlatforms and a Microsoft MVP within the Cloud and Datacenter Management area, where he helps organizations realize the benefits of the hybrid cloud. He is also a co-author of the Microsoft System Center 2012 Service Manager, Orchestrator and Operations Manager cookbooks.

His passion for everything about System Center, Azure and IT systems management reflects through all areas of his work, presentation and day-to-day life in the form of new and innovative solutions brought to market by PowerONPlatforms.

> *This book is dedicated to my wife and family, who are patient enough to put up with me when I get lost for hours, immersed in finding solutions to complex challenges.*

Samuel Erskine is a Systems Management Sr Technical Specialist, Trainer and Author , focused on System Center and MS Cloud technologies. Sam is the content designer and lead author of three Microsoft System Center Cookbooks and co-author of two System Center Unleashed books. He's also a Microsoft MCT , MVP and a regular speaker at community user groups and conferences worldwide.

About the Reviewer

Rafael Delgado is an IT professional with over 12 years of experience and is a cloud management engineer at PowerON. He is currently working across the delivery and development teams, implementing and designing innovative cloud and System Center suite solutions. He spent the majority of his IT career working in local government in a wide range of areas from service desk, desktop support, to third-line infrastructure management. This is the second book he has been a technical reviewer on, previously working on the Microsoft System Center 2016 Service Manager Cookbook.

Rafael is passionate about giving back to the IT community. He also writes a blog that focuses on all things System Center, PowerShell, Azure Automation, Power BI, and more. He is also the creator of the Service Manager and Configuration Manager Power BI dashboards, which can be found on the TechNet gallery. His Twitter handle is @Raf_Delgado.

www.PacktPub.com

For support files and downloads related to your book, please visit www.PacktPub.com.

Did you know that Packt offers eBook versions of every book published, with PDF and ePub files available? You can upgrade to the eBook version at www.PacktPub.com and as a print book customer, you are entitled to a discount on the eBook copy. Get in touch with us at service@packtpub.com for more details.

At www.PacktPub.com, you can also read a collection of free technical articles, sign up for a range of free newsletters and receive exclusive discounts and offers on Packt books and eBooks.

https://www.packtpub.com/mapt

Get the most in-demand software skills with Mapt. Mapt gives you full access to all Packt books and video courses, as well as industry-leading tools to help you plan your personal development and advance your career.

Why subscribe?

- Fully searchable across every book published by Packt
- Copy and paste, print, and bookmark content
- On demand and accessible via a web browser

Customer Feedback

Thanks for purchasing this Packt book. At Packt, quality is at the heart of our editorial process. To help us improve, please leave us an honest review on this book's Amazon page at https://www.amazon.com/dp/1786460467.

If you'd like to join our team of regular reviewers, you can e-mail us at customerreviews@packtpub.com. We award our regular reviewers with free eBooks and videos in exchange for their valuable feedback. Help us be relentless in improving our products!

Table of Contents

Preface

System Center 2016 Orchestrator is an improved version of Opalis, an acquisition of a well-established product by Microsoft. The Opalis product was acquired by Microsoft in 2009 and has seen continual feature updates to its core functionality as well as alignment to the System Center 2016 product's feature offerings.

System Center 2016 Orchestrator (SCO) is a powerful and versatile process automation Information Technology (IT) tool set. SCO provides seamless interconnections between the multiple software products in use in typical IT management environments. This component of the System Center 2016 product uses a graphical workflow creation tool set, and a set of connectors between multiple vendor products known as Integration Packs (IPs) to address its objectives.

The installation and post-installation phases of SCO require you to plan and configure the product in a methodical sequence-based on your requirements. The aim of the book is to address the challenges faced by many first-time users of SCO on how to best plan, deploy, and, more importantly, automate the right processes in their respective organizations. The objective of the authors is to start the reader's journey of Orchestration by sharing valuable insights from real-world scenarios.

The book provides you with independent, task-oriented steps to achieve specific SCO objectives. The authors recommend that you read the first three chapters as a background for subsequent chapters if you are new to SCO and process automation software products. The book may be read in the order of interest, but where relevant, the authors refer to dependent recipes in other chapters.

What this book covers

Chapter 1, *Unpacking System Center 2016 Orchestrator*, provides the steps required to install and configure SCO. This chapter contains recipes on the two installation scenario types for SCO; single-server and multi-server deployments. The objective is to provide the reader with the steps required for installation of SCO in either scenario.

Chapter 2, *The Initial Configuration of SCO 2016*, covers the initial configuration tasks an SCO administrator would need to perform after successfully installing the product. The chapter also delves into deploying and installing Integration Packs.

Chapter 3, *Planning and Creating Runbooks*, delves into the workflow's (Runbooks) planning and designing process for SCO. The planning and designing of Runbooks is a prerequisite for successful value add automation using SCO. This chapter also provides a brief primer to the SCO.

Chapter 4, *Building Advanced Runbooks*, focuses on how to take your SCO Runbooks to the next level. Build a looping Runbook or see how to implement error handling and enable advanced logging.

Chapter 5, *Simple Runbooks for Your Daily Tasks*, covers Runbooks you will need for your Daily Business. We are going step by step through each Runbook, so you will see how to build and understand how these Runbooks work.

Chapter 6, *Advanced Runbooks for Your Daily Tasks*, discusses building advanced Runbooks in your daily business. Each Runbook is an advanced solution and will provide you a rich featured Runbook solution.

Chapter 7, *Doing More with Orchestrator*, provides you a lot of information on how to trigger your SCO Runbooks. One of the best solutions will be in using SCOOSP, a self service portal to trigger your Runbooks.

What you need for this book

In order to complete all the recipes in this book, you will need a minimum of one server configured with System Center 2016 Orchestrator and the relevant interconnecting technologies discussed. Here is the list of technologies the recipes depend on and their relevant versions used for this book:

- Microsoft Active Directory (Windows Server 2008 R2 and above)
- System Center 2016 Configuration Manager
- System Center 2016 Operations Manager
- System Center 2016 Virtual Machine Manager
- System Center 2016 Service Manager
- SCOOSP

The required software and deployment guides for System Center 2016 product can be found at the following official Microsoft website `https://docs.microsoft.com/en-us/system-center/`.

To download SCOOSP, go to `http://bit.ly/SCOOSP_Cookbook`.

The authors recommend using the online Microsoft resource, due to the frequency of updates to the product's supported requirements. Also, note that the dynamic nature of the internet may require you to search for updated links listed in this book.

Who this book is for

The target audience of this book is SCO administrators and process owners responsible for implementing the IT process automation in their respective organizations. The recipes in this book range from beginner level and touches on expert level SCO administration knowledge. The ultimate goal is to provide the reader with knowledge to start their SCO journey, enhance their existing skills, and more importantly to share real-world experience from seasoned technology implementers.

Conventions

In this book, you will find a number of text styles that distinguish between different kinds of information. Here are some examples of these styles and an explanation of their meaning. Code words in text, database table names, folder names, filenames, file extensions, path names, dummy URLs, user input, and Twitter handles are shown as follows: "Create a subfolder called `1.3.1-Delete inactive Computer Accounts`." A block of code is set as follows:

```
$POSTBody = @"
<?xml version="1.0" encoding="utf-8" standalone="yes"?>
<entry xmlns:d="http://schemas.microsoft.com/ado/2007/
08/dataservices"
xmlns:m="http://schemas.microsoft.com/ado/2007/
08/dataservices/metadata" xmlns="http://www.w3.org/2005/Atom">
<content type="application/xml">
<m:properties>
<d:RunbookId type="Edm.Guid">{$($RunbookID)}</d:RunbookId>
```

When we wish to draw your attention to a particular part of a code block, the relevant lines or items are set in bold:

```
$POSTBody = @"
<?xml version="1.0" encoding="utf-8" standalone="yes"?>
<entry xmlns:d="http://schemas.microsoft.com/ado/2007/
08/dataservices"
xmlns:m="http://schemas.microsoft.com/ado/2007/
08/dataservices/metadata" xmlns="http://www.w3.org/2005/Atom">
<content type="application/xml">
<m:properties>
<d:RunbookId type="Edm.Guid">{$($RunbookID)}</d:RunbookId>
```

Any command-line input or output is written as follows:

```
$RetreivedGUID = GetSCOProperty $XML
$RunbookInputProperty "In" "Id"
```

New terms and **important words** are shown in bold. Words that you see on the screen, for example, in menus or dialog boxes, appear in the text like this: "Right click on **Runbook Designers**, and select **Deploy new Runbook Designer**"

Warnings or important notes appear like this.

Tips and tricks appear like this.

Reader feedback

Feedback from our readers is always welcome. Let us know what you think about this book-what you liked or disliked. Reader feedback is important for us as it helps us develop titles that you will really get the most out of. To send us general feedback, simply e-mail feedback@packtpub.com, and mention the book's title in the subject of your message. If there is a topic that you have expertise in and you are interested in either writing or contributing to a book, see our author guide at www.packtpub.com/authors.

Customer support

Now that you are the proud owner of a Packt book, we have a number of things to help you to get the most from your purchase.

Downloading the example code

You can download the example code files for this book from your account at `http://www.packtpub.com`. If you purchased this book elsewhere, you can visit `http://www.packtpub.com/support` and register to have the files e-mailed directly to you. You can download the code files by following these steps:

1. Log in or register to our website using your e-mail address and password.
2. Hover the mouse pointer on the **SUPPORT** tab at the top.
3. Click on **Code Downloads & Errata**.
4. Enter the name of the book in the **Search** box.
5. Select the book for which you're looking to download the code files.
6. Choose from the drop-down menu where you purchased this book from.
7. Click on **Code Download**.

Once the file is downloaded, please make sure that you unzip or extract the folder using the latest version of:

- WinRAR / 7-Zip for Windows
- Zipeg / iZip / UnRarX for Mac
- 7-Zip / PeaZip for Linux

The code bundle for the book is also hosted on GitHub at: `https://github.com/PacktPublishing/Microsoft-System-Center-2016-Orchestrator-Cookbook-Second-Edition`. We also have other code bundles from our rich catalog of books and videos available at: `https://github.com/PacktPublishing/`. Check them out!

Downloading the color images of this book

We also provide you with a PDF file that has color images of the screenshots/diagrams used in this book. The color images will help you better understand the changes in the output. You can download this file from `https://www.packtpub.com/sites/default/files/downloads/MicrosoftSystemCenter2016OrchestratorCookbookSecondEdition_ColorImages.pdf`.

Errata

Although we have taken every care to ensure the accuracy of our content, mistakes do happen. If you find a mistake in one of our books-maybe a mistake in the text or the code-we would be grateful if you could report this to us. By doing so, you can save other readers from frustration and help us improve subsequent versions of this book. If you find any errata, please report them by visiting `http://www.packtpub.com/submit-errata`, selecting your book, clicking on the **Errata Submission Form** link, and entering the details of your errata. Once your errata are verified, your submission will be accepted and the errata will be uploaded to our website or added to any list of existing errata under the Errata section of that title. To view the previously submitted errata, go to `https://www.packtpub.com/books/content/support`and enter the name of the book in the search field. The required information will appear under the **Errata** section.

Piracy

Piracy of copyrighted material on the Internet is an ongoing problem across all media. At Packt, we take the protection of our copyright and licenses very seriously. If you come across any illegal copies of our works in any form on the Internet, please provide us with the location address or website name immediately so that we can pursue a remedy. Please contact us at `copyright@packtpub.com` with a link to the suspected pirated material. We appreciate your help in protecting our authors and our ability to bring you valuable content.

Questions

If you have a problem with any aspect of this book, you can contact us at `questions@packtpub.com`, and we will do our best to address the problem.

1
Unpacking System Center 2016 Orchestrator

In this chapter, we will cover the following recipes:

- Understanding the Orchestrator architecture
- Planning the Orchestrator deployment
- Installing a single server deployment
- Making the Orchestrator environment highly available
- Deploying an additional Runbook Server

Introduction

Microsoft System Center 2016 Orchestrator (SCO) is a process automation and multitechnology product connection toolkit. It delivers the following two key challenges of an organization:

- The automation of manual repeatable tasks
- Connecting multiple IT vendor products

The first common IT challenge, the automation of manual repeatable tasks, when coupled with supporting organization policies, can significantly improve IT value and efficiency. The second challenge, connecting multiple IT vendor products, provides organizations with a single logical product SCO to interconnect and coordinate the activities between the typical multi-vendor technology investments.

In order to deliver the capabilities of SCO, we must unpack the product, our toolbox, by planning our deployment (what is the size, type, and the content of the toolbox) and installing the product based on our agreed deployment plan. This chapter focuses on the activities you must perform to have a fully functional SCO installation.

Understanding the Orchestrator architecture

It is very important to understand the whole architecture of System Center Orchestrator before your start installing any of the SCO components.

Getting ready

The author recommend you to review the latest information on SCO at `https://technet.m icrosoft.com/en-us/library/hh420377(v=sc.12).aspx`, as the documentation about the architecture of the product is regularly updated by Microsoft.

How to do it...

The SCO architecture is made up of six types of components. The basic automated activity delivered by SCO is called a **Runbook**, which is commonly known as workflow in other products. The six components, which make up the SCO product are listed and described in the following table and are illustrated in the figure following the table:

SCO component	Description
The Runbook Designer	The Runbook Designer is a tool used for creating and editing Runbooks. Runbooks are stored in the Orchestration database. A subcomponent of the Runbook Designer is called the Runbook Tester, which is used to validate the execution of Runbooks.
The Orchestration database	The Orchestration database is a Microsoft SQL Server database, which stores Runbooks, the statuses of Runbooks, and the security delegation configuration. The database also stores log files and the configuration of the SCO deployment.

The Management Server	The Management Server is the core communication component of the SCO architecture and is responsible for coordinating the communication between the Runbook Designer and the Orchestration database. There is only one Management Server per SCO deployment.
The Runbook Server	The Runbook Server is responsible for executing the instances of Runbooks. When a Runbook is invoked, a copy of the Runbook instance is sent to its assigned Runbook Server, and then it is executed (by default, this is the first installed Runbook Server, which is assigned the Primary role).
The Orchestrator web service	The Orchestrator web service is the interface that enables applications to connect to SCO. Typical tasks performed through the web service are Runbook status views, start, and stop actions.
The Orchestrator browser console	The Orchestrator browser console is a Silverlight supported web console, which uses the Orchestrator web service to communicate with SCO.

The six parts of SCO are illustrated in the following figure:

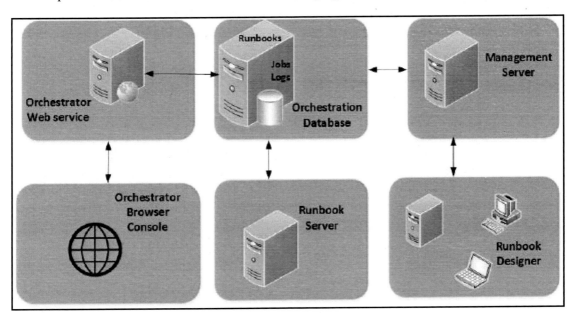

For the smallest implementation, all the components can be deployed to one server (physical or virtual). You have the option to scale out the deployment using multiple servers to host one or more components of SCO. The deployment choice is determined by the planning activities you perform before invoking the installation of the product. This recipe discusses the factors you must consider to assist with the deployment choice.

About the Management Server

 At the time of writing, the current version of SCO supports only one instance of a Management Server per deployment. You can deploy multiple instances of the other parts of the product with a note that we are still dealing with just one database per Management Server. The database instance can be made highly available.

How it works...

The understanding of the SCO architecture is an essential task in order to be successful in automating your task. Before planning your deployment, make sure you understand the architecture and the components of SCO. Afterward, start planning your deployment as described in the recipe, *Planning the Orchestrator deployment*.

Planning the Orchestrator deployment

The installation of SCO is simple. You must plan the deployment appropriately according to your needs. This recipe discusses and provides steps on common planning tasks to be performed before mounting the ISO for organizations who have successfully deployed SCO.

Getting ready

The authors recommend you to review the latest information on SCO at `http://technet.m icrosoft.com/en-us/library/hh420383.aspx`, as the requirements of the product and supported platforms are regularly updated by Microsoft.

How to do it...

There are three planning categories. They are: people, processes, and the technology (SCO product):

1. Identify and agree on the roles and responsibilities of the SCO team. SCO deployments typically have three types of users:

    - **Services accounts**: They perform actions for the specific components of SCO
    - **Administrators:** They will typically perform all the activities including, but not limited to, SCO installation, Runbook creation and management, and the delegation of security to operators
    - **Operators:** They will typically use the SCO console and the Runbook Designer to create and manage Runbooks

2. Identify and document initial prototype processes to be used as the first candidate for automation and testing. The types of processes for this purpose should be simple, repeatable tasks that fall into an organization's required standard service requests. Good candidates are service requests, which do not require authorization and approval. An additional example category is Windows operating system services that can be stopped and started as a part of troubleshooting.

3. Plan for the following technology requirements areas for SCO:

    - **SCO deployment type**:

Deployment type	Description
Single servers	All the SCO roles are installed on one physical or virtual machine. This scenario is typically implemented in test environments but is fully supported in production. This, however, becomes a single point of failure for highly automated environments.
Multiserver	The SCO roles are separated and installed on one or more machines.

- **Minimum hardware requirements for each SCO component:**

Component	Requirements
Management Servers	• Operating system—Windows Server 2016 or Windows Server 2012 R2 • 2 GB minimum • 200 megabytes (MB) of available hard disk space • Dual-core Intel microprocessor, 2.1 gigahertz (GHz) or better • Microsoft .NET Framework 3.5 Service Pack 1
Orchestration databases	• Database: Microsoft SQL 2012 SP2, Microsoft SQL 2014, Microsoft SQL 2014 SP1, Microsoft SQL 2014 SP2, Microsoft SQL 2016 • Collation: SQL_Latin1_General_CP1_CI_AS • Local or remote (Basic Engine only)
Runbook Servers	• Operating system: Windows Server 2016 or Windows Server 2012 R2 • 2 GB minimum • 200 megabytes (MB) of available hard disk space • Dual-core Intel microprocessor, 2.1 gigahertz (GHz) or better • Microsoft .NET Framework 3.5 Service Pack 1
Orchestrator console/web services	• Operating system: Windows Server 2016 or Windows Server 2012 R2 • 2 GB minimum • 200 megabytes (MB) of available hard disk space • Dual-core Intel microprocessor, 2.1 gigahertz (GHz) or better • Microsoft .NET Framework 4.5 with WCF • Web Service: Internet Information Services (IIS) 7.0 and enabled IIS role • Microsoft Silverlight 4**
Orchestrator Runbook Designers	• Operating system: Windows Server 2016 or Windows Server 2012 R2, Windows 10 • 2 GB minimum • 200 megabyte (MB) of available hard disk space • Dual-core Intel microprocessor, 2.1 gigabyte (GHz) or better • Microsoft .NET Framework 3.5 Service Pack 1

- **Services accounts and delegation groups**:

Account/group	Type	Notes
Orchestrator management services	Service accounts	Create an Active Directory user account for this service. This is the main management server service account, and it is granted the "log on as a service" right during the installation.
Orchestrator Runbook monitor services	Service accounts	Typically, this is the same account as the Orchestrator management service.
Orchestrator Runbook services	Service accounts	This is the same user account as the Management and Runbook Server monitor service in a single deployment, but it can be different for multiserver deployments; Active Directory domain account is recommended.
Runbook authors (SCO_ADMINS)	Groups	Create an Active Directory group. This group will have the equivalent access of full administration to the SCO deployment.
Runbook operators (SCO_CON_USERS)	Groups	Create an Active Directory group. This group will have the equivalent access of a Runbook operator to the SCO deployment.
Installation user	User	The user with full administrative rights on the SCO servers is required to perform the installation and configuration of the SCO deployment.

- **Network communication ports:**

Source	Targeted computer	Default port	Configurable
Runbook Designers	Management Servers	135, 1024-65535	Yes, after the SCO Installation.
Management Servers, Runbook Servers, and web services	Orchestration databases	1433	Yes; it is specified during the installation on the SCO supported version of Microsoft SQL Server. This is the case where the SQL Server instance is not using the default port.
Client browsers	Orchestrator web services	81	Yes, during the SCO installation.
Client browsers	Orchestration consoles	82	Yes, during the SCO installation.

How it works...

The planning activities discussed are the minimum activities the authors recommend. The tasks performed at this stage will ensure that you ask and plan for all your requirements before investing time in the actual installation. An additional benefit is identifying any people or budgetary risks before the deployment.

There's more...

There are two additional planning areas, which are typically ignored in technology-focused deployments. These areas are communication strategies and stakeholder management:

- **The communication strategy:** One of the inaccurate myths of SCO is that it would automate the IT professional. SCO, when implemented right, would improve efficiency, but will not replace people. On the contrary, you need to communicate with the people who perform the manual tasks, as they hold the key to how to best automate their efforts. Early engagement with all the IT team members should be one of your key planning tasks.

- **The stakeholder management:** Stakeholders are all users affected by the SCO deployment. An important category of stakeholders is the management team responsible for policy creation and enforcement. Automation without a good planned organization may lead to conflicts at the political level of your organization. An example of such a scenario is the ability to create Active Directory user accounts with rights to specific organization areas and restricted resources.

Installing a single server deployment

This recipe provides the steps required to install all the SCO roles on a single server. The single server deployment is appropriate for test and development environments. This deployment type will assist you with evaluation of the product, initial Runbook creation, and validation prior to deploying in your production environment. Though supported in production, you must plan to implement the multiserver deployment to provide flexibility and availability.

Getting ready

You must plan to review the *Planning the Orchestrator deployment* recipe before performing the steps in this recipe. There are a number of dependencies discussed in the planning tasks, which you must perform in order to be able to successfully complete the steps in this recipe.

The authors assume that you have access to all the installation media, and the user account performing the installation has administrative privileges on the server nominated for the SCO deployment.

How to do it...

The following figure provides a visual summary and order of the tasks you need to perform to complete this recipe:

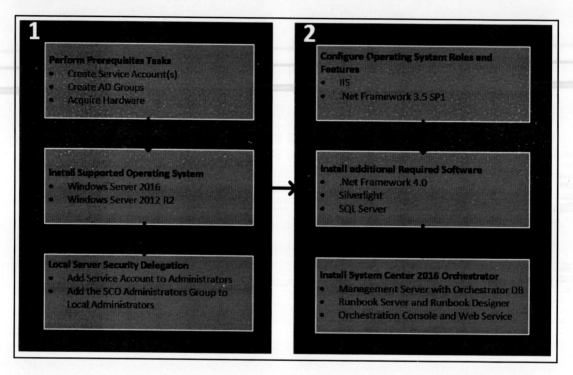

The deployment will be implemented in an Active Directory environment and with the Windows Server 2016 operating system. Perform the following steps to deploy SCO on a single machine:

1. In Active Directory, create the required and recommended user accounts and groups. In this example we will create the following groups:
   - **Users:** SCO_MGTSVCA and SCO_RBSSVCA
   - **Groups:** SCO_ADMINS and SCO_CON_USERS

2. Install a supported Windows Server operating system, and join the server to the Active Directory domain in the scope of the SCO deployment.

3. Add the two services accounts and the SCO Administrators group to the local Administrators group on the SCO server.

4. On the SCO server, enable the following role and feature:
    - **Role**: Web Server (IIS) (default settings) — Note that the installation will enable this role for you if it is not found on the target server
    - **Feature**: .NET Framework 3.5 SP1 — You must specify a source file for .NET Framework 3.5 SP1 in the case of Windows Server 2016, and ensure that the ISO for Windows Server 2016 is loaded

5. Optionally install Silverlight. After the SCO installation, you will be prompted to install Silverlight if you run the console on the server.

6. Install a supported version of Microsoft SQL Server. In our example, we will install Microsoft SQL Server 2016 standard edition. The following are the minimum options required for the installation:
    - **Instance features**: Database Engine Services
    - **Share features**: Management Tools — Basic
    - **Collation**: SQL_Latin1_General_CP1_CI_AS
    - **Authentication Credentials**: Windows Authentication (recommended)

7. Insert or mount the SCO installation media on the server. Login with a user account with administrative rights.

8. Launch the installation using the `SetupOrchestrator.exe` file. Click on **Install** under the **System Center 2016 Orchestrator Setup** section on the wizard page.

9. On the **Product Registration** page, enter your **Organization** details and the **Product Key** (although the product key can be entered post installation, it is a best practice to enter this during the installation to reduce the risk of product evaluation expiry after the default 180 day period). Click on **Next**.

10. Review the **Please read this License Terms** page, and accept to continue with the installation. Click on **Next**.

11. On the **Select features to install** wizard page, ensure all the options are checked. Click on **Next**.

12. On the **Configure the service account** page, type the user account you created for the Management Server service account and password. Click on **Test** to verify the details. Click on **Next**.

13. On the **Configure the database server** page, type the server name, and if applicable, the instance of SQL where the Orchestration database will be created. Click on **Test Database Connection** to verify the connection to the database server. Click on **Next**.

14. On the **Configure the database** page, ensure that **New database** is selected and the default name is Orchestrator for the database. Click on **Next**.

15. On the **Configure Orchestrator users group** page, click on **Browse...** , and specify the Active Directory group you created for the SCO administrators role (SCO_ADMINS in our example). Click on **Next**.

16. On the **Configure the ports for the web services** page, leave default options (81 and 82) or provide your custom options. Make sure you document the custom port if you change the default values. Click on **Next**.

17. On the **Select the installation location** page, accept the selected installation location or specify a custom location. Click on **Next**.

18. On the **Microsoft Update** page, select your preferred option. Click on **Next**.

19. On the **Help improve Microsoft System Center Orchestrator** page, select your preferred options. Click on **Next**.

20. Review the **Installation summary** page. Click on **Install** to start the installation.

21. On successful installation, you are presented with final configuration options as follows:
    - **Launch Windows Update**
    - **Visit System Center Orchestrator Online**
    - **When Setup closes, start the Runbook Designer**

This completes the installation steps.

How it works...

Installing SCO in a single server deployment mode is very simple. The most important aspect is to plan and configure all the prerequisites before you start the actual installation.

The installation requires a number of options, which the wizard guides you throughout the process. The installation creates the Orchestration database and prepares it for use in your deployment. The account specified for the service account is granted the required permission in the database and on the local server.

The following screenshot shows the database permissions granted to the management server service account:

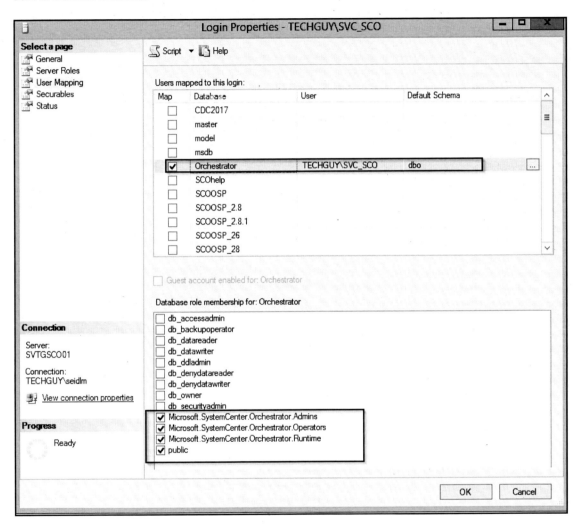

About service accounts

In our prerequisites, we created two service accounts—one for the management service and the other for the Runbook service. In a single server deployment, only one account is requested, which, in our case, is the Management Server service account. The Runbook Server service account will be used for additional Runbook Servers and is a best practice to separate the two accounts, as they are granted different rights in the database. An additional benefit of using two or more accounts is to reduce the risk of a single point of failure for all service components.

There's more...

There is one additional configuration you must perform post installation on the Management Server.

Enabling network discovery is applicable to the Orchestrator database Runbook Designer role. Perform the following steps to enable network discovery:

1. In **Control Panel,** navigate to **Network and Sharing | Change advanced sharing settings,** and expand the domain profile and **Turn on network discovery**.
2. Click on **Save changes**.

Enabling network discovery enables the auto-population of fields, which requires the selection of a computer name when creating Runbooks.

See also

The official online documentation is updated regularly and should be a point for reference at: `https://docs.microsoft.com/en-us/system-center/orchestrator/learn-about-orchestrator`.

Making the Orchestrator environment highly available

SCO features and components can be installed on a single server or across multiple servers. All SCO components can be installed multiple times, except the Management Server. The Management Server and his SQL database can only exist a single time in an Orchestrator environment.

Getting ready

To understand the Orchestrator role, see the recipe, *Understanding Orchestrator architecture*, in this book.

If you would like to make your SCO environment highly available, prepare your server like you did it for the first Instance.

How to do it...

There are different ways for each feature to make them highly available. Runbooks Server, web service, the Orchestration console, and Runbook Designer can be installed multiple time in your environment. The Management Server feature is not that easy to make highly available. See next how to make each feature highly available.

Runbooks can be configured to run on a single Runbook Server or fallback to a different one, see recipe, *Making your Runbook highly available*, `Chapter 4`, *Building Advanced Runbooks*.

The Runbook Designer can be installed multiple times on a Server or client OS, as they are completely standalone and are used to connect to a Management Server.

The Orchestration console and web service can also be installed multiple times; you only need to take care about the web service URLs and make them highly available with DNS and SPN.

To make the Management Server highly available, you need to take care about the OS and the DB itself.

Here is a list about your options in this:

- Make the OS highly available, for example, as a VM on a cluster
- Take care of the SQL database also as a VM on a cluster

At the time this book has been written, it is not supported to run a System Center Orchestrator database on a SQL *Always ON* instance.

How it works...

As you see, the Management Server is not that easy to be highly available, and it is a very important information. It's related to the SCO architecture, that all the information is stored in the database, so the DB is very important to to your complete SCO environment.

See also

Check out the *How to do it…* section of the *Planning the Orchestrator deployment* recipe.

Deploying an additional Runbook Server

SCO features and components can be installed on a single server or across multiple servers. The multiserver deployment requires you to perform the installation in a specific order. The first server you must install is the Management Server, which requires a supported instance of Microsoft SQL Server. This recipe discusses the installation of the Runbook Server component. You need at least one Runbook Server in a multiserver deployment.

Getting ready

You must plan to review the *Planning the Orchestrator deployment* recipe before performing the steps in this recipe. There are a number of dependencies in the *Planning the Orchestrator deployment* recipe, which you must perform in order to successfully complete the tasks in this recipe.

The authors assume that you have access to all the installation media; and the user account performing the installation has administrative privileges on the server nominated for the SCO deployment. You must also install a Management Server before you can install the Runbook Server.

The example deployment in this recipe is based on the following configuration details:

- Management Server and database server called SVTGSCO01 is already installed
- The service account created in Active Directory: SCO_RBSSVCA

How to do it...

The following figure provides a visual summary and order of the tasks you need to perform to complete this recipe:

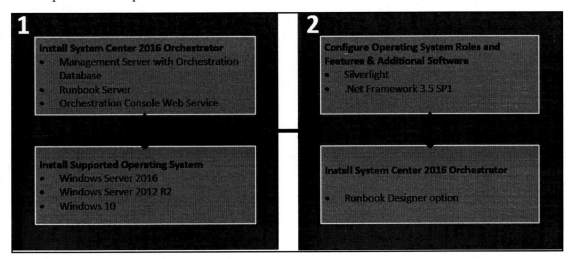

The deployment will be implemented in an Active Directory environment with the Windows Server 2016 operating system. Perform the following steps to deploy SCO Runbook Server in a multiserver deployment:

1. Install a supported Windows Server operating system, and join the server to the Active Directory domain in the scope of the SCO deployment.
2. Add the service accounts and SCO administrators group to the local administrator's group on the SCO Runbook Server.
3. On the SCO server, enable the .NET Framework 3.5 SP1 feature.
4. Insert or mount the SCO installation media on the server. Login with a user account with administrative rights.
5. Launch the installation using the SetupOrchestrator.exe file.

6. Turn on the splash screen under Standalone installations. Click on **Runbook Server**.

7. On the **Product Registration** page enter your **Organization** details and the **Product Key**. Click on **Next**.

8. Review the **Please read this License Terms** page and click **accept** to continue with the installation. Click on **Next**.

9. On the **Configure the service account** page, type the user account you created for the Runbook Server service account and password (in our scenario, SCO_RBSSVCA). Click on **Test** to verify the details. Click on **Next**.

10. On the **Configure the database server** page, type the server name, and if applicable, the instance of SQL where the Orchestration database is installed. Click on **Next**.

11. On the **Configure the database** page, ensure that **Existing database** is selected and the default name is Orchestrator, or your custom name for the database is selected. Click on **Next**.

12. On the **Select the installation location** page, accept the selected installation location or specify a custom location. Click on **Next**.

13. On the **Microsoft Update** page, select your preferred option. Click on **Next**.

14. On the **Help improve Microsoft System Center Orchestrator** page, select your preferred options. Click on **Next**.

15. Review the **Installation summary** page. Click on **Install** to start the installation.

16. On the successful installation, you are presented with final configuration options as follows:
      - **Launch Windows Update**
      - **Visit System Center Orchestrator Online**

This completes the installation steps for the SCO Management Server in the multiserver deployment.

How it works...

The installation wizard guides you through the required settings. Once all the prerequisites are properly configured, the installation process installs the required program files for the Runbook Server feature.

The account specified for the service account is granted the required permission in the database. The following screenshot shows the database permissions granted to the Runbook Server service account:

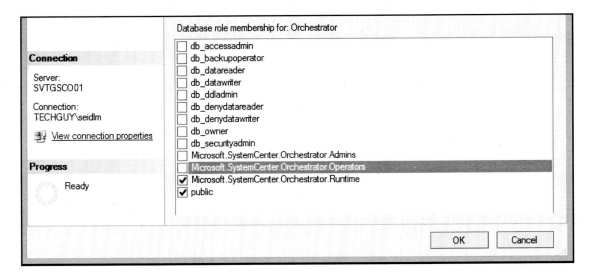

See also

The *How it works...* sections of the following recipes provide additional relevant information:

- Installing a single server deployment recipe
- Installing a Management Server in a multiserver deployment recipe

The Initial Configuration of SCO 2016 2

In this chapter, we will cover the following topics:

- Deploying an additional Runbook Designer
- Registering an SCO Integration Pack
- Deploying the IP to Designers and Runbook Servers
- The initial Integration Pack configuration
- Creating and maintaining a security model for Orchestrator

Introduction

The recipes in Chapter 1, *Unpacking System Center 2016 Orchestrator*, discuss setting up the System Center 2016 Orchestrator environment and how to make it highly available. This chapter will show you how to set up an Orchestrator environment and how to deploy and configure Orchestrator Integration Packs.

Deploying an additional Runbook Designer

The recipes in Chapter 1, *Unpacking System Center 2012 Orchestrator*, discuss deploying SCO in a single or scaled mode. In either case, you can scale out further after the initial deployment.

The Runbook Designer is the key Feature to build your Runbooks. After the initial installation, Runbook Designer is installed on the Server. For your daily work with Orchestrator and Runbooks, you have to install the Runbook Designer on your client or on an Admin Server. We will go through these steps in this recipe.

Getting ready

You must review the *Planning the Orchestrator deployment* recipe from Chapter 1, *Unpacking System Center 2016 Orchestrator*, before performing the steps in this recipe. There are a number of dependencies in the planning recipe that you must perform in order to successfully complete the tasks in this recipe.

You must install a Management Server before you can install the additional Runbook Designers. The user account performing the installation has administrative privileges on the server nominated for the SCO deployment, and it must also be a member of OrchestratorUsersGroup or have equivalent rights.

The example deployment in this recipe is based on the following configuration details:

- Management Server called TLSCO01 with a remote database is already installed
- System Center 2016 Orchestrator

How to do it...

The Runbook Designer is used to build Runbooks using standard activities and/or Integration Pack activities. The designer can be installed on either a server class operating system or a client class operating system.

The *Installing a Single Server Environment* recipe in Chapter 1, *Unpacking System Center 2016 Orchestrator*, discusses and provides steps for the installation using the SCO media.

Follow these steps to deploy an additional Runbook Designer using the deployment manager:

1. Install a supported operating system and join the Active Directory domain in the scope of the SCO deployment. In this recipe, the operating system is Windows 10.

2. Ensure you configure the allowed ports and services if the local firewall is enabled for the domain profile. See the link for details, https://technet.micros oft.com/en-us/library/hh420382(v=sc.12).aspx.

3. Log in to the SCO Management Server with a user account with SCO administrative rights.

4. Launch System Center 2016 Orchestrator **Deployment Manager**:

5. Right-click on **Runbook Designers**, and select **Deploy new Runbook Designer**:

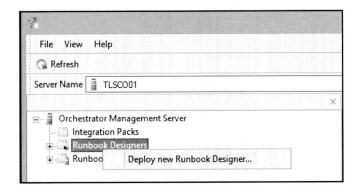

6. Click on **Next** on the welcome page. Type the computer name in the **Computer**: field and click on **Add**. Click on **Next**.

7. On the **Deploy Integration Packs or the Hotfixes** page, check all the Integration Packs required by the user of the Runbook Designer (for this example, we will select the AD IP).

8. Click on **Next**. Click on **Finish** to begin the installation using the Deployment Manager.

How it works...

The Deployment Manager is a great option for scaling out your Runbook Servers and also for distributing the Runbook Designer without the need for the installation media. In both the cases, the Deployment Manager connects to the Management Server and the database server to configure the necessary settings. On the target system, the Deployment Manager installs the required binaries and optionally deploys the Integration Packs selected.

Using the Deployment Manager provides a consistent and coordinated approach to scale out the components of an SCO deployment.

See also

The https://docs.microsoft.com/en-us/system-center/orchestrator/ official web link is a great source of the most up to date information on SCO.

Registering an SCO Integration Pack

Microsoft System Center 2016 Orchestrator (SCO) automation is driven by process automation components.

These process automation components are similar in concept to a physical toolbox. In a toolbox, you typically have different types of tools, which enable you to build what you desire. In the context of SCO, these tools are known as **Activities**.

Activities fall into two main categories:

- **Built-in Standard Activities:** These are the default activity categories available to you in the Runbook Designer. The standard activities on their own provide you with a set of components to create very powerful Runbooks.
- **Integration Pack Activities:** Integration Pack Activities are provided either by Microsoft, the community, solution integration organizations, or are custom created by using the Orchestrator Integration Pack Toolkit. These activities provide you with the Runbook components to interface with the target environment of the IP. For example, the Active Directory IP has the activities you can perform in the target Active Directory environment.

This recipe provides the steps to find and register the second type of activities into your default implementation of SCO.

Getting ready

You must download the Integration Pack(s) you plan to deploy from the provider of the IP. In this example, we will be deploying the Active Directory IP, which can be found at `https://www.microsoft.com/en-us/download/details.aspx?id=54098`.

You must have deployed a System Center 2016 Orchestrator environment and have full administrative rights in the environment. Review `Chapter 1`, *Unpacking System Center 2016 Orchestrator*, if you have not deployed the SCO environment.

How to do it...

We will deploy the Microsoft **Active Directory (AD) Integration Pack (IP)**.

The Integration Pack organization

A good practice is to create a folder structure for your Integration Packs. The folders should reflect versions of the IPs for logical grouping and management. The version of the IP will be visible in the console and as such you must perform this step after you have performed the step to load the IP(s). This approach will aid in change management when updating IPs in multiple environments.

Follow these steps to deploy the Active Directory Integration Pack:

1. Identify the source location for the Integration Pack in scope (for example, the AD IP for SCO2016). Download the IP to a local directory on the Management Server or UNC share.

2. Log in to the SCO Management server. Launch the Deployment Manager:

3. Under Orchestrator Management Server, right-click on Integration Packs. Select **Register IP with the Orchestrator Management Server**:

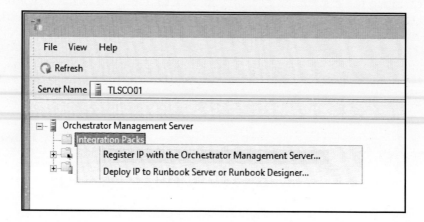

4. Click on **Next** on the welcome page. Click on **Add** on the **Select Integration Packs or Hotfixes** page. Navigate to the directory where the target IP is located, click on **Open**, and then click on **Next**:

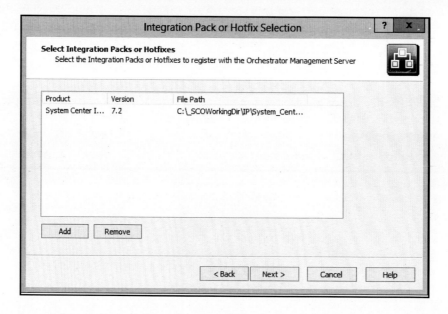

5. Click on **Finish**. Click on **Accept** on the *End-User License Agreement* to complete the registration. Click on **Refresh** to validate whether the IP has successfully been registered.

How it works...

The process of loading an Integration Pack is simple. The prerequisite for successfully registering the IP (loading) is ensuring you have downloaded a supported IP to a location accessible to the SCO Management Server. Additionally, the person performing the registration must be an SCO administrator.

At this point, we have registered the Integration Pack to our Deployment Wizard; two steps are still necessary before we can use the Integration Pack; see the following recipe for this.

There's more...

Registering the IP is the first part of the process of making the IP activities available to Runbook Designers and Runbook Servers. The next step has to be the deployment of Integration Packs to Runbook Designer. See the next Recipe for this.

Orchestrator Integration Packs are provided not only by Microsoft but also third-party companies such as Cisco or NetAPP are providing OIP's for their products. Additionally, there is a huge community that are providing Orchestrator Integration Packs.

There are several sources for downloading Integration Packs, here are some useful links.

- http://www.techguy.at/liste-mit-integration-packs-fuer-system-center-orchestrator/
- http://scorch.codeplex.com/
- https://www.microsoft.com/en-us/download/details.aspx?id=54098

Deploying the IP to Designers and Runbook Servers

Registering the Orchestrator Integration Pack is only the first step; you also need to deploy the OIP to your Designer or Runbook Server.

Getting ready

You have to follow the steps described in the *Registering an SCO Integration Pack* recipe before you can start with the next steps to deploy an OIP.

How to do it...

In our example, we will deploy the Active Directory Integration Pack to our Runbook Designer.

Follow these steps to deploy the Active Directory Integration Pack.

Once the IP in scope (AD IP in our example) has successfully been registered, follow these steps to deploy it to the Runbook Designers and Runbook Servers:

1. Log in to the SCO Management Server and launch **Deployment Manager**:

2. Under Orchestrator Management Server, right-click on the Integration Pack in scope and select Deploy IP to Runbook Server or Runbook Designer:

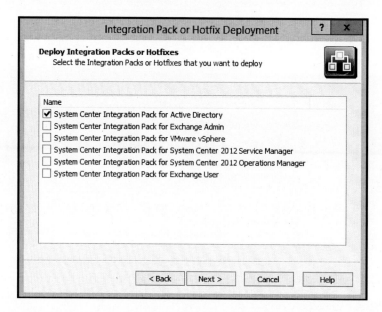

3. Click on **Next** on the welcome page, select the IP you would like to deploy (in our example, **System Center Integration Pack for Active Directory**), and then click on **Next**.

4. On the computer selection page, type the name of the Runbook Server or Designer in scope, and click on **Add** (repeat for all servers in the scope). On the Installation Options page, you have the following three options:

  - **Schedule installation**: Select this option if you want to schedule the deployment for a specific time. You still have to select one of the next two options.
  - **Stop all running Runbooks before installing the Integration Packs or Hotfixes**: This option will, as described, stop all current Runbooks in the environment.
  - **Install the Integration Packs or Hotfixes without stopping the running Runbooks**: This is the preferred option if you want to have a controlled deployment without impacting current jobs:

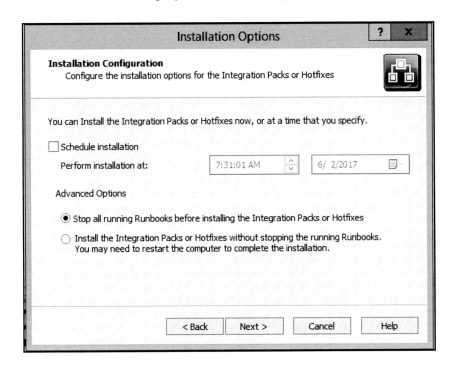

5. Click on **Next** after making your installation option selection. Click on **Finish**.
6. The Integration Pack will be deployed to all selected Designers and Runbook Servers. You must close all Runbook Designer consoles and relaunch to see the newly deployed Integration Pack.

How it works...

The process of deploying an Integration Pack is simple. The prerequisite for successfully deploying the IP (loading) is ensuring you have registered a supported IP in the SCO Management Server.

Now that we have successfully deployed an Orchestrator Integration Pack, if you have deployed it to a Runbook Designer, make sure you close and reopen the Designer to be able to use the activities in this Integration Pack. Now that your are able to use these activities to build your Runbooks, the only thing you have to do is to follow the next recipe and configure this Integration Pack.

The steps can be used for each single Integration Pack; you can also deploy multiple OIP with one deployment.

Now you will be able to use the newly deployed Integration Packs and activities in your Runbooks.

There's more...

You have to deploy an OIP to every single Designer and Runbook Server where you want to work with the activities. It doesn't matter if you want to edit a Runbook with the Designer or want to run a Runbook on a special Runbook Server, the OIP has to be deployed to both.

With Orchestrator Deployment Manager, this is an easy task to do.

The initial Integration Pack configuration

This recipe provides the steps required to configure an Integration Pack for use once it has been successfully deployed to a Runbook Designer.

Getting ready

You must deploy an Orchestrator environment and also deploy the IP you plan to configure to a Runbook Designer before following the steps in this recipe.

The authors assume that the user account performing the installation has administrative privileges on the server nominated for the SCO Runbook Designer.

How to do it...

Each Integration Pack serves as an interface to the actions SCO can perform in the target environment. In our example, we will be focusing on the Active Directory connector. We will have two accounts under two categories of AD tasks in our scenario:

IP name	The category of actions	The account name
Active Directory	Domain Account Management	SCOAD_ACCMGT
Active Directory	Domain Administrator Management	SCOAD_DOMADMIN

The following diagram provides a visual summary and order of the tasks you need to perform to complete this recipe:

...

Follow these steps to complete the configuration of the Active Directory Integration Pack options in the Runbook Designer:

1. Create or identify an existing account for the IP tasks. In our example, we are using two accounts to represent two personas of a typical Active Directory delegation model. SCOAD_ACCMGT is an account with the rights to perform account management tasks only, and SCOAD_DOMADMIN is a domain admin account for elevated tasks in Active Directory.

2. Launch the Runbook Designer as a SCO administrator, select **Options** from the menu bar, and select the IP to configure (in our example, **Active Directory**):

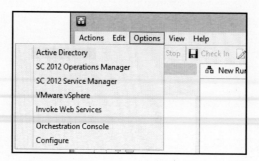

3. Click on **Add**, type `AD Account Management` in the **Name:** field, and select `Microsoft Active Directory Domain Configuration` in the **Type** field by clicking on the **...** button.
4. In the Properties section, type the following:
    -   **Configuration User Name**: `SCOAD_ACCMGT`.
    -   **Configuration Password**: Enter the password for `SCOAD_ACCMGT`.
    -   **Configuration Domain Controller Name (FQDN)**: The FQDN of an accessible domain controller in the target AD (in this example, `TLDC01.TRUSTLAB.LOCAL`).
    -   **Configuration Default Parent Container**: This is an optional field. Leave it blank:

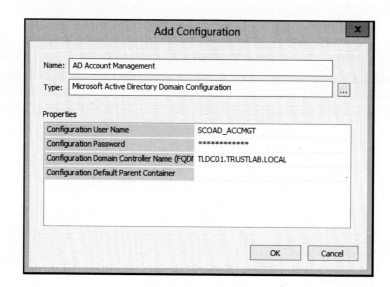

5. Click on **OK**. Repeat steps 3 and 4 for the domain admin account, and click on **Finish** to complete the configuration.

How it works...

The Integration Pack configuration is unique for each system environment that SCO interfaces with for the tasks in scope of automation. The Active Directory IP configuration grants SCO the rights to perform the actions specified in the Runbook using the activities of the IP.

Typical Active Directory activities include, but are not limited to creating user and computer accounts, moving user and computer accounts into organizational units or deleting user and computer accounts.

In our example, we created two connection account configurations for the following reasons:

- Follow the guidance of scoping automation to the rights of the manual processes. If we use the example of a Runbook for creating user accounts, we do not need domain admin access. A service desk user performing the same action manually would typically be granted only the account management rights in AD.
- We have more flexibility with delegating management and access to Runbooks. Runbooks with elevated rights through the connection configuration can be separated from Runbooks with lower rights using folder security.

The configuration requires the planning and understanding of its implication before implementing.

Each IP has its own unique options, which you must specify before you create Runbooks using the specified IP. The default IPs that you can download from Microsoft include the documentation on the properties you must set.

There's more...

As you have seen in this recipe, we need to configure each additional Integration Pack with a connections string, user, and password. The built-in activities from SCO are using the service account rights to perform these actions, or you can configure a different user for most of the built-in activities. This we will see in `Chapter 3`, *Planning and Creating Runbook Designs*, in the *Creating a Runbook* recipe.

Creating and maintaining a security model for Orchestrator in this chapter expands further on the delegation model in SCO.

See also

The official online documentation for Microsoft Integration Packs is updated regularly and should be a point for reference at: `https://www.microsoft.com/en-us/download/details.aspx?id=54098`.

Creating and maintaining a security model for Orchestrator

Microsoft System Center 2016 Orchestrator provides you with the ability to delegate and secure components in its infrastructure. The process to create this security model differs from some of the other System Center family of products. In this recipe, we will discuss and provide steps to configure a security model using a real world scenario.

Getting ready

You must have a fully deployed System Center 2016 Orchestrator environment in order to complete this recipe.

Security model scenario

In our example environment, we have five roles in scope for our initial security configuration:

- SCO Full administrators
- SCO Default Web Console Users
- SCO Runbook Designer Users
- SCO Active Directory Runbook Designers
- SCO Active Directory Console Users

The following table describes the roles and their relevant assigned Active Directory groups:

Organization role	Active Directory group	Members	Description
SCO Full administrators	`SCO Admins`	It has the SCO infrastructure administrator users. Note that members will have elevated privileges via Runbooks.	Have access to all Runbooks and is the equivalent of an Active Directory domain and enterprise admins roles.
SCO Default Web Console Users	`SCO_CON_USERS`	It has all the users requiring access to the Orchestration console. In this example, it will also include `SCO_ADCON_USERS`.	User group with minimum rights to the Orchestration console (no Runbooks available).
SCO Runbook Designer Users	`SCO_RBD_USERS`	All the users requiring access to connect to the Management Server with a Runbook Designer in this example the group will also include `SCO_ADRBD_USERS`.	User group with minimum rights to connect the Runbook Designer to the management server.
SCO Active Directory Runbook Designers	`SCO_ADRBD_USERS`	Users are nominated as AD Runbook designers.	Administrators with access to standard activities and the AD IP for Runbook creation and administration.
SCO Active Directory Activities Console Users	`SCO_ADCON_USERS`	Users are nominated as AD Runbook executors and monitors with the Orchestration console.	Users with access to run AD Runbooks using the Web Console.

How to do it...

The security model implementation will be split into five configuration categories.

Preparing and organizing the environment

Consider the following table:

Node/subnode	Folder/subfolders	Description
Runbooks	Root	This creates top-level global Runbooks here.
Runbooks	1-Cookbook \1.1-Chapter4	This creates AD Runbooks here.
Computer Groups	Root	This creates top-level global computer groups here.
Global Settings\Counters	Root	This creates top-level global Counters here.
Global Settings\Variables	Root	This creates top-level global Variables here.
Global Settings\Schedules	Root	This creates top-level global Schedules here.

We will follow these steps to create an initial folder structure for security delegation using the preceding table as our guide:

1. Log in to a SCO Runbook Designer computer with a user account with SCO administrative rights, and connect to the Management Server.
2. Select the Runbooks node. Right-click on the Runbooks folder and select **New | Folder**. Type Root as the folder name.
3. Repeat the folder creation steps for the nodes specified in the preceding table.

Configuring DCOM permissions

We will follow these steps to assign the DCOM security delegation using the security scenarios table. You must create the AD groups before you perform the steps in this recipe:

1. Log into a SCO Management Server computer with a user account with SCO administrative rights.

2. Go to **Control Panel | Administrative Tool**. Launch **Component Services**. Expand the **Component Services** node and then expand **Computers**. Right-click on **My Computer** and select **Properties**.

3. Select the **COM Security** tab. Under **Access Permissions**, click on **Edit Limits, Under Group,** or **user names:** box. Click on **Add** and Select the AD groups nominated as general access for Console Users and Runbook Designers (in our example, SCO_CON_USERS and SCO_RBD_USERS). Click on **OK**.

4. Select the AD group you added, and check **Local Access** and **Remote Access** in the **Allow** column. Click on **OK**.

5. Ensure you are still on the **COM Security** tab. Under **Launch and Activation,** click on **Edit Limits, Under Group** or **user names:** dialog box, click on **Add**, and select the AD groups nominated as general access for Console Users and Runbook Designers (in our example, SCO_CON_USERS and SCO_RBD_USERS). Click on **OK**.

6. Select the AD groups in turn, and check **Local Launch, Remote Launch, Local Activation,** and **Remote Activation** options in the **Allow** column. Click on **OK** twice.

7. In the **Component Services** node, expand **Computers**. Go to **My Computer | DCOM Config,** and scroll down to **management**. Right-click on it and select **Properties**.

8. Click on **Security** tab. Under **Launch and Activation Permissions**, click on **Edit,** and then click on **Add**. Select the AD groups nominated as general access for Console Users and Runbook Designers (In our example, **SCO_CON_USERS** and **SCO_RBD_USERS**). Click on **OK**.

9. Select the AD groups in turn and check **Local Launch, Remote Launch, Local Activation,** and **Remote Activation** in the **Allow** column; and click on **OK** twice.

10. Under **Access Permissions**, click on **Edit,** and then click on **Add**. Select the AD groups nominated as general access for Console Users and Runbook Designers (in our example, SCO_CON_USERS and SCO_RBD_USERS). Click on **OK**.

11. Select the AD groups in turn and check **Local Access** and **Remote Access** in the **Allow** column. Click on **OK** twice, and close the **Component Services** node

12. Run the **Services** applet. Restart the Orchestrator Management Service.

Designer and console delegation

Follow these steps to give general access to the Runbook Designer and Orchestration console. In our example, we will grant the minimum access required to the two groups SCO_CON_USERS and SCO_RBD_USERS:

1. Log in to a SCO Runbook Designer computer with a user account with SCO administrative rights and connect to the Management Server.
2. Select the Runbooks node, right-click, and select **Permissions**. Click on **Add**. Select the groups in scope; select each group in turn. Uncheck all permissions except **Read**. Click on **Advanced**. Select each of the groups you added in turn and click on **Edit**. In the **Applies to:** field, select **This object only**. Click on **OK** three times to apply the setting.
3. Repeat step 2 for the following node and subnodes:
   - **Computer Group**s
   - **Global Settings\Counters**
   - **Global Settings\Variables**
   - **Global Setting\Schedules**
4. Select the Runbook Servers node, Right-click and select **Permissions**. Click on **Add**. Select the groups in scope. Select each group in turn. Uncheck all the permissions except **Read**, and click on **OK**.

This completes the configuration for general access to the Designer and Orchestration console.

Configuring AD IP Runbook permissions

In our example, 1-Cookbook/1.1-Chapter 4 contains our AD Runbooks, so follow these steps to grant access to this folder for members of your AD Group:

1. Log in to a SCO Runbook Designer computer with a user account with SCO administrative rights, and connect to the Management Server.
2. Navigate to the Runbooks parent folder. Repeat the steps in the Designer and Console Delegation section to grant read only access to the Cookbook parent folder only in our example (selection applies to This object only in the Advanced permissions).

3. Navigate to the folder or sub folder under the Runbooks node (1–Cookbook\1.1–Chapter 4 in our example). Right-click on the folder and select **Permissions**. Click on **Add** and select the Group nominated for the designer delegation (in our case SCO_ADRBD_USERS). Click **OK** and then **Advanced**. Select the group you added and click **Edit**, and then click **Show advanced permissions**, configure the permissions, and click **OK** when complete.

4. Repeat step 2 for the nominated Orchestration Console group (in our example, SCO_ADCON_USERS, but only select the console required permissions (**Read Properties**, **Write Properties**, **List Contents**, and **Publish**).

Restricting options by Runbook Designer Integration Pack deployment

In our scenario, we will install the SCO Runbook Designer on a workstation called TLWSCO02 for a SCO delegated administrator responsible for creating and maintaining AD related Runbooks. The Designer will only have standard activities and the AD Integration Pack. Follow these steps to deploy a designer with the AD IP using Deployment Manager:

1. Follow the steps in the recipe *Deploying Runbook Servers and Designers with the Deployment Manager*. Only select the AD IP for our workstation (TLWSSCO02).

2. Once completed, log into the Designer workstation with the user in the SCO_ADRBD_USERS group.

3. Connect to the SCO Management Server using the Runbook Designer on TLWSSCO02, and validate the user access to Runbooks and the options section.

Note that all folders are visible, but a user without permission to the folder will get an *access denied* message, as shown in the following screenshot:

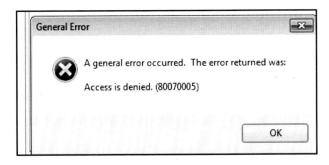

How it works...

The security framework in SCO requires that you grant access to the Management Server and the top-level folders or nodes before users can traverse to specific subfolders. The Runbook Designer by default has four system nodes: Runbooks, Computer Groups, Runbook Servers, and Global Settings. We have the ability to manually create securable objects under the root of the Runbooks, Computer Groups, and Global Settings.

The recipe is split into four sections, which you must plan to complete in order to grant the right level of access in an organized and maintainable manner.

Using top-level folders and default groups ensures that, at minimum, users can connect to the console and Management Server without the risk of executing or modifying existing Runbooks.

A further delegation using local Runbook Designers with only the IPs relevant to the users ensures that the general options, which cannot be hidden will not be available (for example, the options for the VMware IP is not required by a user delegated for AD Runbook creation).

Using separate groups for the Orchestration console provides you with additional flexibility and reduces access to the Designer for administrators responsible for only executing Runbook (for example, a user creation Runbook assigned to the service desk team will only require Orchestration console access).

There's more...

As seen in this recipe, you can configure your SCO Environment to fit nearly every Security need in your environment. But, it is not necessary every time to implement role-based access to SCO. At many companies, Orchestrator is used by a very small group of IT Admins, mostly 1-2. This group is doing the whole automation tasks for the whole company, so they have access to Active Directory, Exchange, System Center, and everything else.

So, this is also a way to use Orchestrator in your Environment, to have a small group of Full SCO admins, who are using every Integration Pack and building every Runbook.

Additionally, a lot of Runbooks, mostly the complex ones like user on-boarding, require access to multiple systems and require to talk to different Offices in your company to define the process and automate this with Runbooks. And this is most of the time easier when done by a small group of admins.

As you see, you can fit Orchestrator Security Concept to your company needs. Just make sure you think about this before making and building your first Runbooks.

See also

The `https://docs.microsoft.com/en-us/system-center/orchestrator/runbook-permissions`link provides additional information on SCO security delegation.

3
Planning and Creating Runbooks

In this chapter, we will cover the following recipes:

- Initial steps to consider before creating a Runbook
- Making Runbook scenarios automation ready
- Documenting Runbook designs
- Understanding the Orchestrator scenario building blocks
- Runbook Designer standards and primer
- Creating a Runbook

Introduction

Moving from manual processes to automation leads to the following questions:

- Is automation the root of all **Information Technology (IT)** evil?
- Is the lack of automation the root of IT evil?

The answer to both the questions is "it depends". In most circumstances, we can say yes to either question. So "evil" may sound a little strong for technology; however, this is similar to the view of money. There is a definite fact that a lack of a well-defined and optimized process is the root of any automation evil. This chapter discusses steps we can take to ensure that the Runbooks (process workflows) we implement in System Center 2016 Orchestrator meet our needs as intended without the introduction of inefficient automation.

Initial steps to consider before creating a Runbook

The Microsoft **System Center 2016 Orchestrator (SCO)** automation is implemented with what is known as Runbooks. Runbooks help us implement manual tasks using a workflow approach.

This recipe provides example steps to identify candidates for SCO automation.

Getting ready

The key to a successful conversion of a manual process to a semi or fully automated process is a clear understanding of what you are trying to automate. A recognized method for describing the manual process is the use of stories better known as scenarios. Scenarios typically involve one or more stakeholders responsible for the ownership and execution of the process. You must plan to involve all the stakeholders of the scenarios you plan to automate using SCO. At a minimum, you must involve the owner of the process.

How to do it...

The following figure provides a visual summary and the order of the tasks you need to perform to complete this recipe:

Let's go through these three steps and see what to do.

Identifying scenarios

This is an important step because you need to find tasks you can automate. Between ourselves, *Everything can be automated* but it should make sense, honestly.

So, how can we find tasks to automate?

At the first appointments at my customers, talking about Automation, customers already have some ideas about what they want to have automated. Additionally, I tell the customer some examples from our experience about what we already have automated.

But the most effective way I have figured out in the past years is to ask people in charge of their manual task, for example, your service desk team, your infrastructure admins, your exchange admins, your server admins, and so on.

Try to explain them how they can save time and make their processes more reliable, and they will have lots of ideas and will tell them unasked.

So, let's see how you can identify your scenarios:

- Ask yourself, what I am doing every day, week, and monthly as a manual task
- What manual task is your team doing on a regular basis
- Ask your IT Colleagues about their manual tasks
- Ask yourself, your team, and colleagues what they think can be automated
- See the next list about some Runbook Examples
- don't be afraid to question WHY they are doing that manual task, sometimes a task can be left there from a historical point and no longer even relevant.

Here are just a few Runbooks to start with:

- User on boarding
- User off boarding
- User changes
- A reboot server
- A set out of office reply
- An automated client install
- Find the next free computer name
- Set exchange full access
- VM provisioning

And there are a lot more such examples.

Validating and agreeing

Now, you have found a lot of tasks to automate, but how to decide which one you should automate?

Just a note, automating a task is not only to save time; it is also important for your quality. So, the quality of your tasks will get better with automation. Keep this in mind whenever you need to choose your task to automate.

So, how to decide which task should be automated? At the beginning of an automation project, a *quick win* makes it easier to understand the benefits of automating your tasks.

As a *user on boarding* can be a very complex task, maybe it is not the best way to start with. To set an *out of office reply* is an easy task and a typical *quick win*.

When you have made a decision about the task to automate, see the following steps on how to proceed.

Here is an example of the steps you must perform to prepare for Runbook implementations:

1. Create a list of requested or identified manual repeatable tasks.
2. For each task, ask and document the answers to the following questions:
   - Who is the owner of the task?
   - How is the task done today?
   - Who is responsible for performing this task?
   - How long does it take to perform the task?
   - Is the task susceptible to errors/omissions?
   - Is the desired outcome consistent?
   - Does the task require input from another task(s)?
   - Do other tasks depend on the output of this task?
3. Identify and document all the users and systems involved with the current manual task.
4. Discuss and agree on the tasks to be automated based on the information captured in the document.
5. The value of automation is a business and technological balance. Plan to involve the business decision makers in the selection of candidates for automation. Also if possible back your decisions up with facts like service desk stats showing biggest issues which could highlight quick wins.

Optimizing and documenting

The previous steps lead you to the last one, to optimize and document your automated task.

You have all the necessary information about the task you want to automate and how the process looks like actually. Now, it's time to think about how to automate all this steps, and in this phase, it mostly happen that you and your team figure out to optimize some steps.

This is also a benefit of automating your task; your process will be reflected, and there is always some space left for improvement. Use this opportunity and increase the quality of your process.

And don't forget to document everything, the original process, the new process, and the reasons why you have changed the process.

How it works...

Automation requires you to identify the right candidates of manual tasks based on the actual need and value to your business. Typical scenarios maybe identified as a result of business requests for efficiency or maybe even due to a proactive analysis of current processes and time taken to execute. The series of questions will help you identify the right value and risks associated with automating the tasks.

These questions also capture the task owners and interfaces on which the task depends and/or which depends on the task.

The process will require formal and informal discussions. The outcome should be documented and agreed before proceeding to the SCORCH Runbook design.

A very important factor to understand is that Runbook designing, building, testing, and ongoing maintenance will also incur additional cost. A good candidate for automation should be able to positively offset the automated solution investment. An example of a bad candidate is a scenario similar to the insight from Anders Asp (MVP).

The task you plan to automate takes a manual effort of 30 minutes from one person per week. This equates to 26 hours a year (0.5 x 52 weeks). If the effort to create a Runbook to automate this task takes 80 hours to build, this scenario is not a good candidate, as it would take more than 3 years to get a **Return on Investment (ROI)**.

A good candidate for SCO would be to plan automating eight manual tasks, which take 15 minutes each to complete every week. If the effort to create a Runbook to automate this task takes 5 hours to build, this scenario is a good candidate as it would provide an ROI after 2.5 months.

Making Runbook scenarios automation ready

This recipe provides the steps required to prepare a manual process for automation.

Getting ready

You must plan to review and perform the steps in the *Initial steps to consider before creating a Runbook* recipe.

How to do it...

Perform the following steps to prepare each scenario for automation:

1. Create a flowchart of the steps to be executed in the scenario.
2. Identify the task's steps. which can be performed without requiring any approval.
3. Identify tasks, which require approval and categorize into two sections:
    - **A pre-approval by the authorized requester**: The initial request is from an authorized source or person
    - **An approval required at execution**: A step requires approval before proceeding
4. To execute the tasks, split each manual task in the scenario into mini independent tasks. The mini tasks should serve as the smallest unit of the blueprint for a Runbook.
5. Combine the mini tasks in the sequence in which the overall scenario is executed. Stop the combination at the approval required steps.
6. Each approval step should be a check point to create a separate Runbook with the input from the current Runbook.
7. A separate event triggered inputs from human initiated inputs. Map the inputs to the mini tasks.

How it works...

The steps defined and discussed in the recipe provide a method to optimize a chosen scenario for automation. The objective you want to achieve is to remove the need for human intervention. If the task steps require human approval or input, then you cannot achieve full automation with SCO. Your aim is to ensure that each Runbook can complete the given expected set of inputs.

The final result should be similar to a specification with known inputs, processing steps, and the expected outputs of each task.

Documenting Runbook designs

This recipe is a continuation of the first two recipes of this chapter. The *Initial Steps to Consider before Creating a Runbook* recipe discusses identifying the right candidates for automation. The *Making Runbook scenarios automation ready* recipe provides steps on taking the scenario and optimizing it for the automation with SCO. This recipe completes the loop with a discussion and example on documenting a real scenario.

Getting ready

You must plan to review and perform the steps in the *Initial Steps to Consider before Creating a Runbook* recipe and the *Making Runbook scenarios automation ready* recipe.

How to do it...

We will use the following scenario to discuss the steps in this recipe.

Scenario

You have a business requirement to automate the creation of new employee user accounts in Active Directory. Perform the following steps to document the design for the scenario:

1. Use this table to capture inputs, outputs, authorization, and notes in the process steps:

Scenario artifact	Value	Additional notes
Input	Human resources requests	This can be a single user request or multiple requests using a text file.
Authorization and approval	Implied in the requests	This is a standard domain account, so the authorization is in the request.
System/technology for task execution	Active Directory	Permission right to create a user account.
Output	Enabled user account with initial random password	The user account must be created with a flag to change password on first logon.
Output format	Print out of details	Print out details and provide to authorized new user.

2. Create a flowchart to represent the desired Runbook to implement the manual steps. The aim of the flow chart is to capture the three core areas and their dependent parts as shown in the following figure (**Inputs**, **Processing**, and **Outputs**):

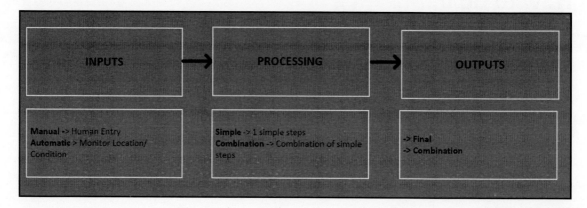

3. Using our scenario example and the preceding figure as a guide, the flowchart or your preferred documentation tool would have the following aspects:

- **Inputs**: This provides the required user details to Orchestration Console or a file with a list of formatted user details within a specified accessible network location
- **Processing**: This is an automated series of user creating steps (create user, set password, and enable)
- **Outputs:** This sends details to output channel(s) through a console, e-mail, or printer

How it works...

The documentation process approach discussed serves as a guideline and a high-level template. SCO is a very powerful tool, which shares similar characteristics with software programming languages. Documenting the design will save you a great deal of time and frustration; you will have the opportunity to walk through the steps before investing time in the Runbook Designer console.

SCO Runbooks are self-documenting once created, but the logic and thoughts behind the final Runbook are not. This approach is similar to creating manual maps before converting to a satellite navigation system.

See also

- Runbooks in `Chapter 5`, *Simple Runbooks for Your Daily Tasks*, and Chapter 6, *Advanced Runbooks for Your Daily Tasks*.

Understanding the Orchestrator scenario building blocks

This recipe provides a brief overview of SCO basics and serves as a primer for `Chapter 4`, *Building Advanced Runbooks* to Chapter 6, *Advanced Runbooks for your Daily Tasks* . Unlike other recipes, the focus of this recipe is on you understanding it instead of performing. This recipe is, however, equally important, as you will need an understanding of the SCORCH basics in order to create the recipes in the book.

Getting ready

You must have a fully deployed SCO environment. Your environment should have a database server, Management Server, Runbook Server, Runbook Designer, and an orchestration web console. Chapter 1, *Unpacking System Center 2016 Orchestrator*, discusses and provides steps on how to install and configure a typical SCO environment.

How to do it...

The basic terms you need to be familiar with and their description are as detailed in the following table:

Orchestration term	Description
Activities	These are the building blocks of an Orchestrator workflow, which are known as Runbooks. There are two types, standard and custom activities.
Standard activities	These are the default installation activities visible in the Runbook Designer.
Custom activities	These are the activities you get from deploying an Integration Pack. An example is the Active Directory integration pack, which provides Active Directory activities such as create a user or computer.
Integration Pack (IP)	A bundle of activities for interfacing with the target environment/technology. These can be vendor/third-party solutions, or you can create your own with the toolkit.
Runbook	This is a single unit of a process workflow in Orchestrator. The Runbook will have one starting point (input) and a series of steps with decision points and outputs.
Link (intelligent links)	Links connect two activities in a Runbook. Links are intelligent, because they have configurable properties and conditional logic on how to proceed to the next step.
Monitors	An input activity, which monitors a condition, for example, an event log entry type or a file location.
Trigger	This refers to starting (input) a Runbook based on a monitored condition or as a result of the output of another Runbook

Orchestration term	Description
Counters	This is a global object you configure and use in Runbooks with looping activities (for example, you may create a counter to repeat a process for a fixed number of times before proceeding to the next step).
Schedules	This is used to create a shared global date and time value to use in multiple Runbooks. For example, some activities may only be performed within defined maintenance windows.
Variables	Variables are of a global nature, for example, defining a variable for shared drive or a computer name of a target environment.
Check Out	This is the process of marking a Runbook for exclusive editing. You must check out the Runbook from the database before you edit it in the Runbook Designer.
Check In	This is the converse of check out. You check in the Runbook to save your changes to the Orchestration database, and make it available for execution.
Published Data	The properties of each activity, either at runtime or generic, are made available to other activities using what is known as a databus. These runtime or generic properties are known as published data.
Subscribe	The process of using information from either the databus (published data) or global data like counters, variable, and schedules.
Databus	This is the Orchestration mechanism, which holds the data from activities. Subsequent activities or links may use the information from the databus as their inputs.
Job	A queue of jobs is created for Runbooks pending execution. Runbook Servers check this queue and execute the relevant job.
Instance	When a Runbook is executing on a Runbook Server, it is known as an instance. More than one instance of the Runbook can be executed on the same Runbook Server or multiple Runbook Servers.
Pipelining	How you move from one activity to another based on the link conditions.

Plan to review the official online documentation for SCORCH, which is continually updated by Microsoft for the latest information.

There's more...

The process of creating, testing, and running the automation of scenarios (Runbooks) is managed by three feature areas of SCO.

The three main feature areas you will typically be working within the SCO product are here:

- The Runbook Designer console
- The Runbook Tester component
- The Orchestration web console

A tour of the Runbook Designer

1. Here are the basics of the Runbook Designer console showing the four main panes in the following screenshot:

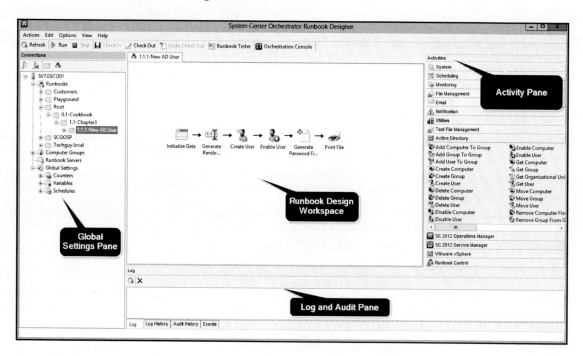

2. You drag the arrow from one activity to the other to create the link. Once the link is created (arrow headed line), you double-click on it to configure its properties. The following screenshot is as an example of a link:

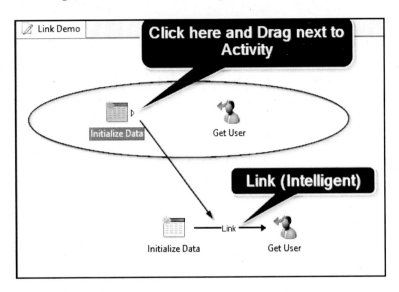

3. You double-click on the link to configure its properties and also see what sort of published data is available for the next activity:

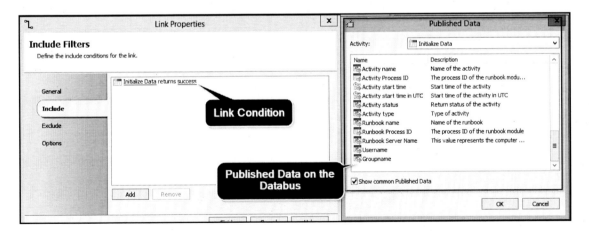

A tour of Runbook Tester

You invoke the Runbook Tester component from the Runbook Designer console. You are prompted to check out the Runbook in scope if you have not done this already. Here are the basics of the Runbook Tester shown in the following screenshot:

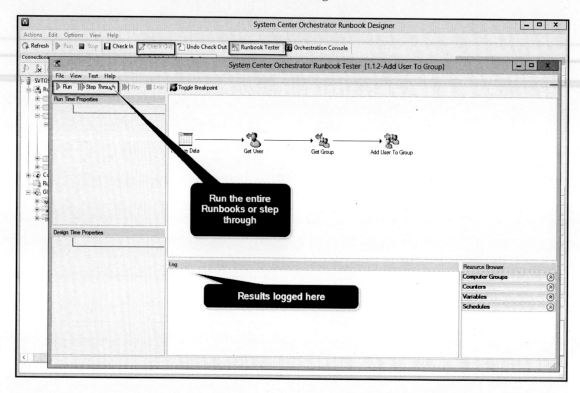

Runbooks run in the Tester much slower than in normal, but it is important to validate the actual processing speed in normal operation.

The Runbook Tester caution

The **Runbook Tester** is not a simulator. It would perform the actual activity in the Runbook. For example, if the Runbook deletes a user account, then the action will be performed on the specified account. You use the tester to validate actual execution. In our example, you will have to create a dummy account nominated for testing in order not to impact a real account. A better practice is to test in a development environment and exports your validated Runbooks into a production environment. Additionally, the **Runbook Tester** executes in the context of the user who

TIP launched the tester. If your automation depends on a system/elevated account; then your tests will have to include a preproduction phase of letting the actual Runbook execute without the use of the tester (use the web console).

The Orchestration web console

You use the Orchestration web console to manually invoke Runbooks and monitor executing Runbooks.

This is effectively an Orchestrator operations role web console. An administrator will use the Designer to create a Runbook, test it with the Runbook Designer, and make it available to Operators who use the Orchestration web console.

Following is the screenshot of the Orchestration web console:

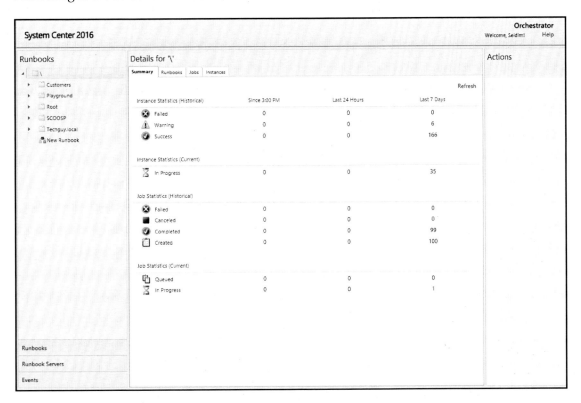

Runbook Designer standards and primer

This recipe provides you with introductory information on the Runbook Designer activities you must perform to create your Runbooks. The recipe also discusses current standard practices when working with the System Center 2016 Orchestrator component.

Getting ready

The requirements for this recipe is a fully deployed SCO environment and a user with administrative access to the Runbook Designer. The example provided uses the *System Center Configuration Manager* Integration Pack.

How to do it...

This recipe is categorized as follows:

- How to standardize your activity configuration
- Check in and check out
- Working with custom and common published data bus parameters

How to standardize your activity configuration

Here are some general rules you can follow to standardize your SCO environment:

1. Create folder structures in the Runbook Designer. The structures must reflect how you intend to manage and delegate Runbooks. Examples include Runbook folders based on the automation process or the Integration Pack type.
2. Create a naming convention for your Runbooks and ensure you rename your activities.
3. The general rule for Runbook directions are from left to right. You can work from top to bottom and then left to right
4. Color code the links between Runbooks. An example is to use green for successful actions and red for failures. The choice is yours but have a standard!
5. Create test Orchestrator Runbooks targeted at test environments.

Check in and check out

System Center 2016 Orchestrator Runbooks are stored in the Orchestration database. When you edit Runbooks, you have to check out the Runbook. The check out is effectively taking a copy of the Runbook and marking the Runbook in the database as read only. No one can edit that specific Runbook until a **Check In** action is performed.

Here are the steps you must follow to check out a Runbook:

1. In the Runbook Designer, select the **Runbooks** (tab name) in the middle pane.
2. Right-click on the tab for the Runbook you want to check out and select **Check Out**.

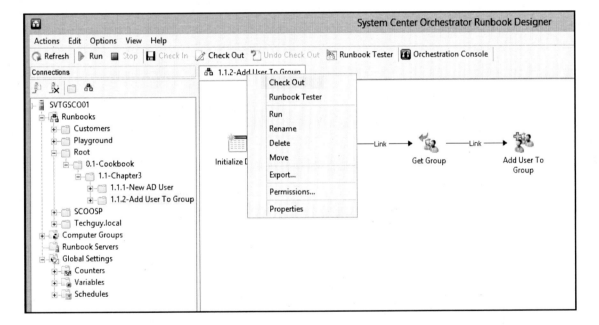

3. When you complete the Runbook configuration, you must **Check In** the Runbook. Here are the steps to **Check In** the Runbook.
4. In the Runbook Designer, select the **Runbooks** (tab name) in the middle pane.

5. Right-click on the tab for the Runbook you want to check in and select **Check In**.

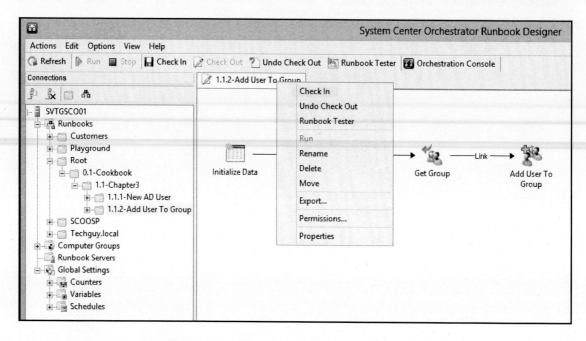

6. You can also use the Buttons in the menu bar:

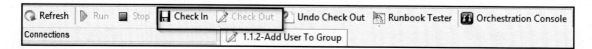

Working with custom and databus parameters

There are three common parameter types you will typically use in Runbook:

*   Basic custom parameter
*   Parameters from previous activities
*   Common published data

An example of configuring a basic parameter is the use of the **Initialize Data** activity. For example, if you need the user to provide a name for a collection that you intend to create with automation, follow the following steps:

1. Double-click on your Initialize activity, and select the **Details** tab.
2. Click on **Add** and click on the underlined **Parameter 1** (this is the default value, which you must rename).
3. Type your custom parameter name and click on **OK**.

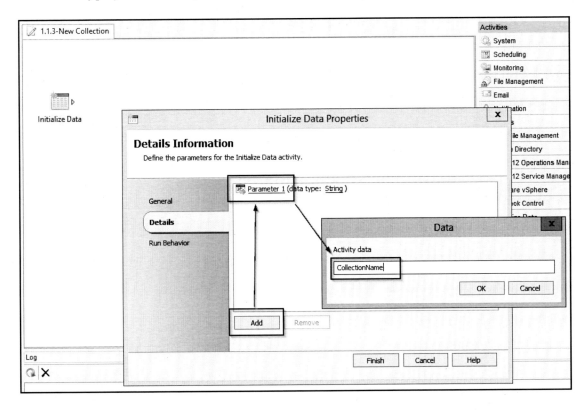

The second type of parameter is what you have available from the data bus from a previous activity. If you add a **Create Collection** activity from the Configuration Manager IP, you can use the **Subscribe** to **Published Data** steps to access the first custom parameter as follows:

1. Double-click on the activity (for example, **Create Collection activity**), select the **Details** tab, and select the configuration for **ConfigMgr**.

2. Right-click on the **Collection Name** field, and navigate to **Published Data |
Subscribe | Initialize Activity**. Your parameter from the previous activity is
available for selection:

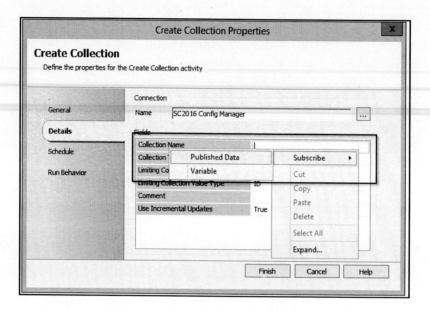

Select the **CollectionName** from **Initialize Data**:

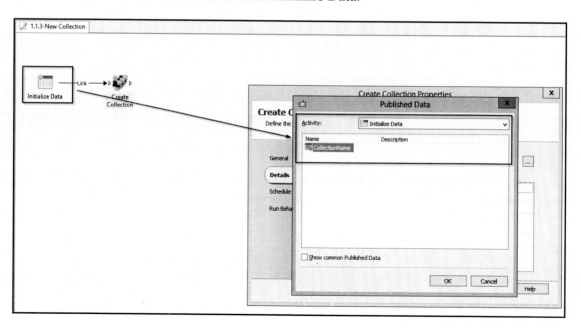

3. The third type of parameter is what you generally get from the data bus. These parameters are typically Runbook meta data information, for example, the name of the Runbook. You may want to use this type of information in notifications (Runbook name). You must follow these steps to view and subscribe to common **Published Data** parameters.

4. Double-click on the activity (for example, **Create Collection activity**), and select the **Details** tab. Select the configuration for **ConfigMgr**.

5. Right-click on the **Comment** field and select **Subscribe | Published Data |** check **Show common Published Data**. Here, additional dynamic parameters, such as Runbook name, are available for selection:

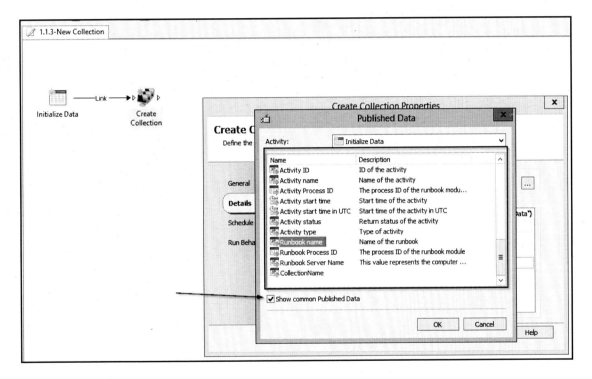

How it works...

The information provided in this recipe is a primer for the Runbooks you will create as you follow the recipes in Chapter 4, *Building Advanced Runbooks*, through to Chapter 4. Use this chapter as a baseline guide and adjust to suit your specific environment.

There's more...

You have additional options to simplify the process of configuring activities. One of the valuable options to be aware of is the expand field.

Expanding parameter fields

The fields in the Runbook designer can be expanded to provide a clearer view of the data you type or the data you subscribe to from the data bus. Simply right-click on the field, and select **Expand** to view all the data. The **Expand** option is particularly useful when you must type scripts or construct comments, which span more than one line:

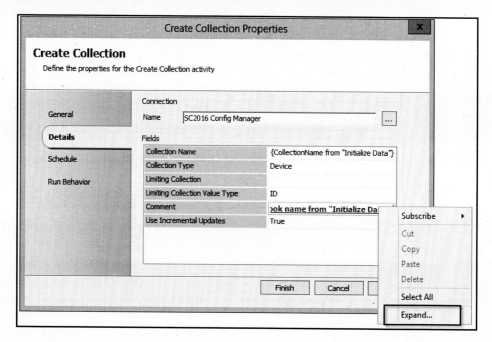

Enter the following in the expanded Window:

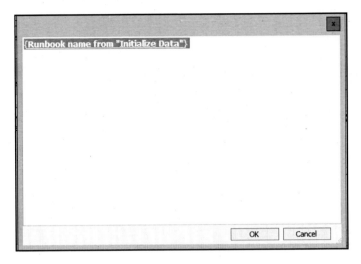

See also

The best and most up-to-date resource on Orchestrator basics is the official Microsoft link for the product at `https://docs.microsoft.com/en-us/system-center/orchestrator/`.

Creating a Runbook

This recipe will show you how to build your first Runbook. It is very important that you follow the recipe, step by step to complete your first Runbook. In this recipe we will create a Runbook to create a user.

Getting ready

For this recipe, it is very important to have gone through the previous recipe in this chapter, otherwise repeat. Now, we will build our first Runbook.

How to do it...

In this Recipe, you are going to learn how to build an Ad-Hoc Runbook and a Monitoring Runbook. Please note that we are using a special naming convention on Folders and Runbooks.

For Example, our Root Folder is named 0-Root the Fist Subfolder is named 0.1-Active Directory and so on. Also the Runbooks are following this naming convention. So it is much easier to find your Runbook, cause you will have a lot of them if your start working with SCO

Building an Ad-Hoc Runbook

An Ad-Hoc Runbook is a Runbook, which will triggered as needed and to some stuff. In our example, we are creating an Active Directory user.

As you learned in a previous Recipe, we are starting with a write done of our Runbook; see our Process here:

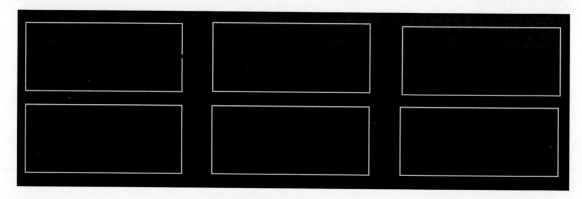

Honestly, this is a very simple user On boarding, but it is a very good example for our fist Runbook. Let's go:

1. Open your Runbook Designer, navigate to your the Root\0.1-Cookbook\ 1.1-Chapter3 folder we created before, and a right-click on **New...** and **Folder**:

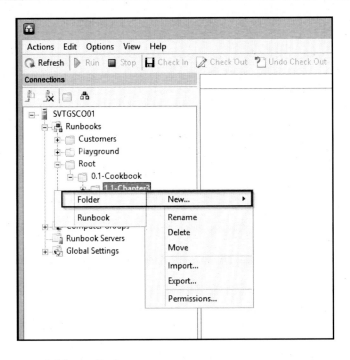

2. Create a new folder called `1.1.1-New AD User`.

3. Right-click on the newly created folder, and click on **New...** and **Runbook**:

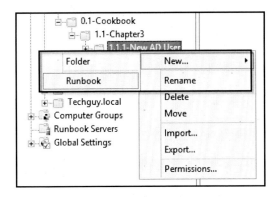

4. Name the Runbook like the folder `1.1.1-New AD User`.

5. Now, we should see an empty Runbook ready to go:

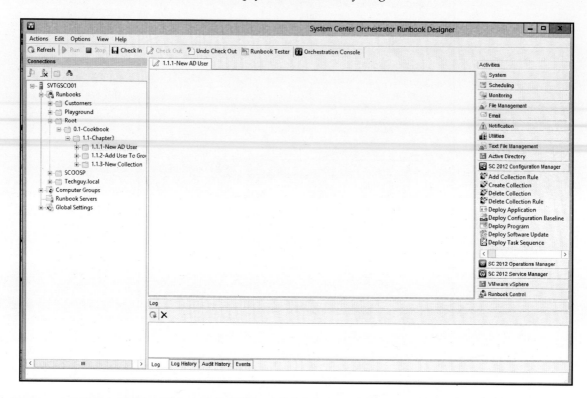

6. First, drag and drop an **Initialize Data** activity from the Runbook control group:

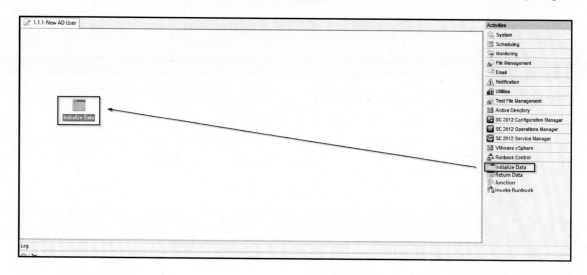

7. Right-click on the **Initialize Data** activity and click on **Properties**:

8. Like we have defined in the beginning, add four parameters and name them correctly:

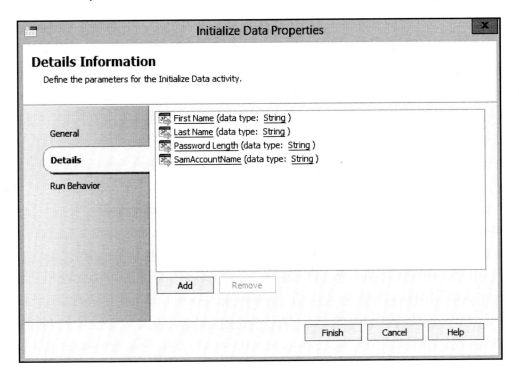

9. The next activity will generate a password for us, so navigate to **Utilities** and choose the **Generate Random Text** activity:

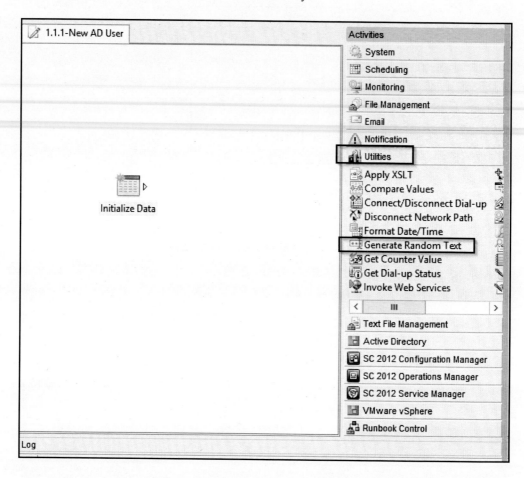

10. Link the **Initialize Data** activity and the new **Generate Random Text** activity:

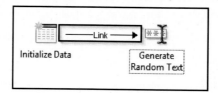

11. Go to the **Properties** page of the **Generate Random Text** activity.

12. This activity will be used to generate a Password, so name the Activity like this. Go to the **General** tab, and type in `Generate Password`:

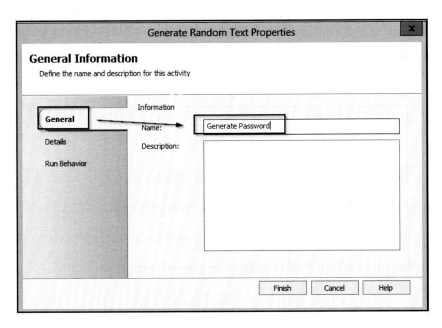

13. Switch to the **Details** tab; here we can configure the basic settings of the activity:

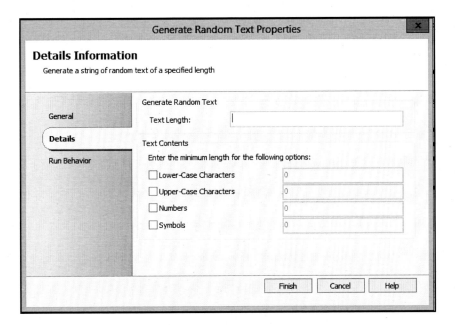

14. The property, **Text Length,** is a setting we define with the Initialize Data, so let's start with it.

15. Right-click on the field, and click on **Subscribe** and **Published Data**:

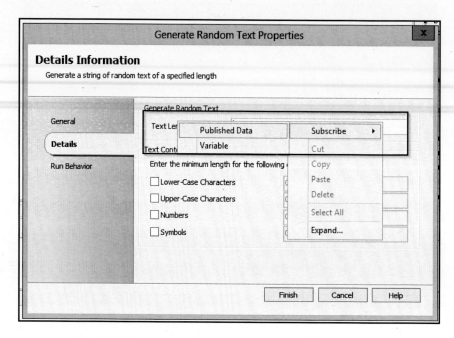

Choose the **Password Length** here:

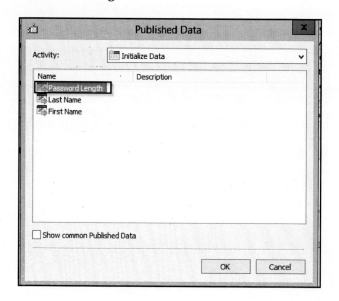

16. The other options can be configured like this:

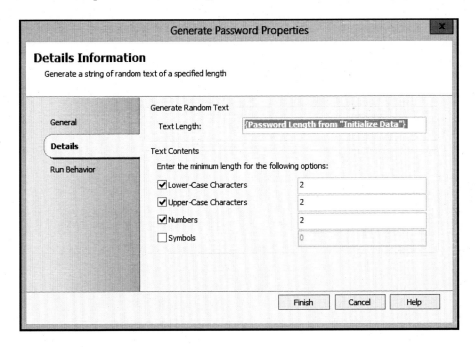

17. The next activity should be **Create User** from the **Active Directory** group:

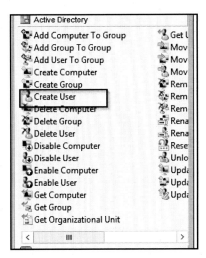

18. Drag it to your Runbook and open **Properties**.
19. First, we have to configure the connection, so choose your Active Directory config:

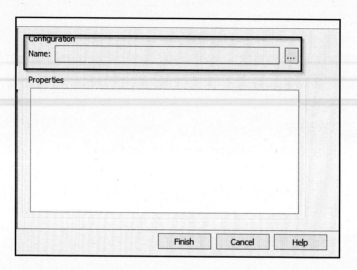

20. Next, just add some more Properties to be filled:

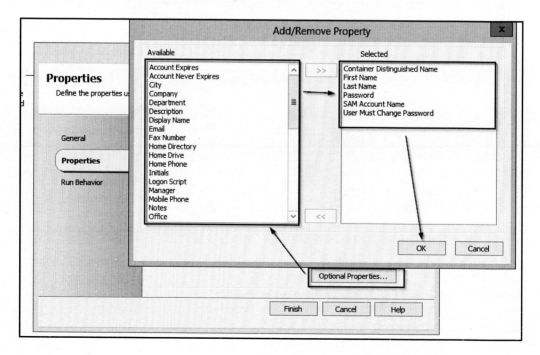

21. Last, we need to fill some values in our **Properties** by subscribing to Published Data or typing the values:

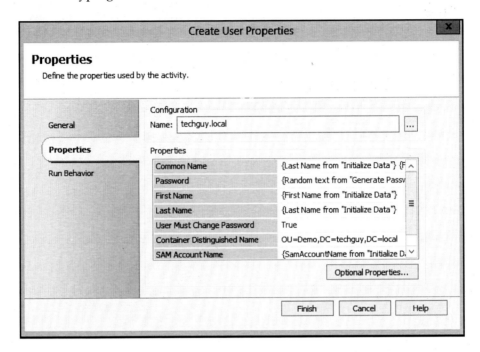

22. The next activity needs to be **Enable User** from the **Active Directory** group:

23. Connect the new activity to the activity **Create User,** and set **Properties** like this:

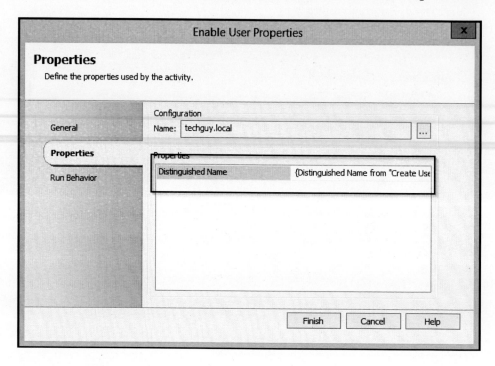

24. Here's a short summary of our Runbook so far to make sure you have the same Runbook like me:

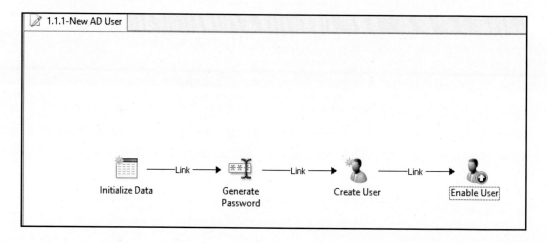

25. The next step will be to add the **Append Line** activity from **Text File Management**:

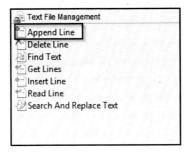

26. Let's see the properties and configure like that, first we need to choose a target where to store the file. I have named the file like the `SamAccountName from "Initialize Data"`:

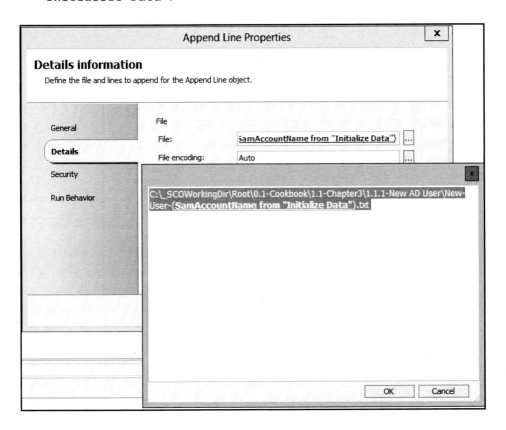

27. The text I have configured like this, feel free to change:

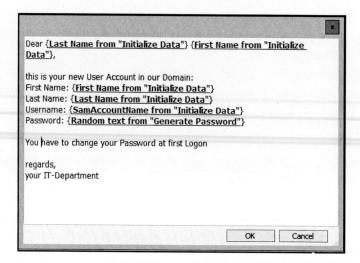

28. The last activity in our Runbook will be the **Print File** from File Management:

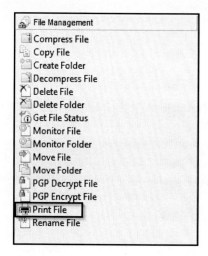

29. Configure the properties as you see in the screenshot:

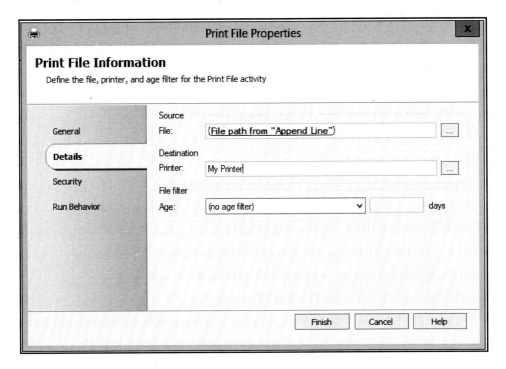

30. Lastly, **Check In** your Runbook to save your work:

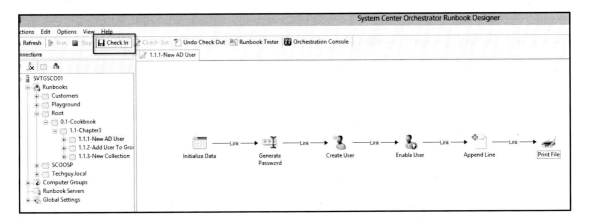

Building a monitoring Runbook

A monitoring Runbook is different from the Ad-Hoc Runbook we built before. The major difference is a monitoring Runbook is always running and is triggering the activities when a special condition occurs.

In this example, we will build a monitoring Runbook to monitor a service state and write an event log when the service stops:

1. Open your Runbook Designer and navigate to your Root\0.1-Cookbook\ 1.1-Chapter3 folder that we have created before; and right-click on the **New...** and **Folder**:

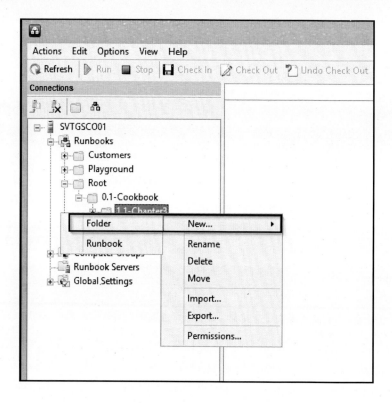

2. Create a new Folder called **1.1.4-Monitor Service**.

3. Right-click on the newly created folder, then click on **New...** and **Runbook**:

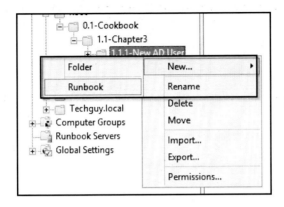

4. Name it like the folder, `1.1.4-Monitor Service`:

5. So, let's start with our new Runbook, and drag the **Monitor Service** activity from **Monitoring**:

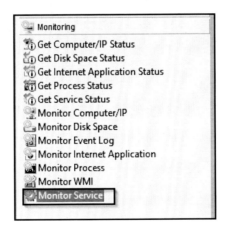

6. Let's see what kind of properties we need to define:

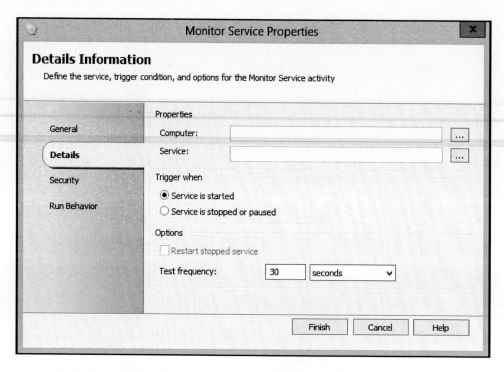

7. For the Computer Property, let's select a server where we can also test our monitoring Runbook. for the Service I will select **Printer Spooler**. I want a Runbook that will get triggered if a service is stopped or paused.

8. So, make sure **Properties** look like this:

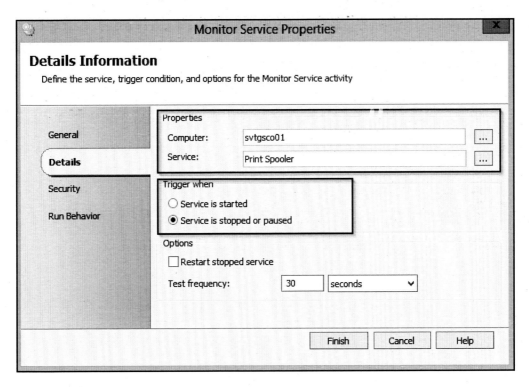

9. All the following activities will be triggered when the conditions are met, so let's drag the **Send Event Log Message** activity from **Notification**:

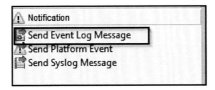

10. Configure the properties similar to this:

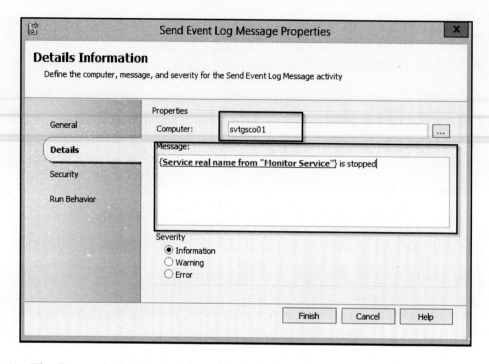

11. The Runbook should look like this:

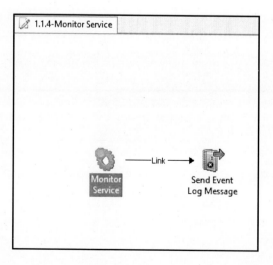

12. Check in your Runbook and start.

How it works...

As you see, the Runbook will be in Running mode, but nothing's happened:

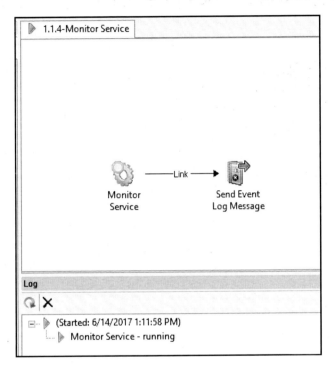

If you will now try to stop the Spooler Service, the Runbook will be fired and will produce an entry in the log history in your Runbook Designer. It will also make an event log message such as we configured the Runbook.

Still, the Runbook will keep running and is waiting for the next trigger to occur.

There's more...

It is very important to understand the difference between Ad-Hoc and Monitoring Runbooks and when to use what. Also understand that a monitoring Runbook is not really a solution to replace something such as SCOM.

4
Building Advanced Runbooks

In this chapter, we will be providing recipes on how to build advanced Runbooks in Microsoft System Center 2016 Orchestrator:

- Creating a child Runbook
- Building a looping Runbook
- Implementing logging in your Runbook
- Implementing error handling in your Runbook
- Making your Runbooks highly available

Introduction

What you have seen in `Chapter 3`, *Planning and Creating Runbook Designs*, was just the beginning on how to build a Runbook. In this chapter, we will see how to build some more advanced Runbooks. Read this chapter carefully, as this will take your automation to the next level.

You have to complete the previous chapters to successfully archive the steps in this chapter.

Creating a child Runbook

Creating a child Runbook is one of the most essential tasks in SCO. Technically, there is no difference between *normal* Runbooks and a *child* Runbook.

A child Runbook is a Runbook with initialized data and often return data and is mostly used for tasks that are needed by multiple Runbooks.

For example, a Runbook, which is adding a user in the AD Group can be a child Runbook, as this task is often used by different Runbooks.

So, it makes sense to build one Runbook, such as a module PowerShell programming, with all the features you need, instead of building the task in each Runbook separately.

See this chart for a better understanding of how a child Runbooks works:

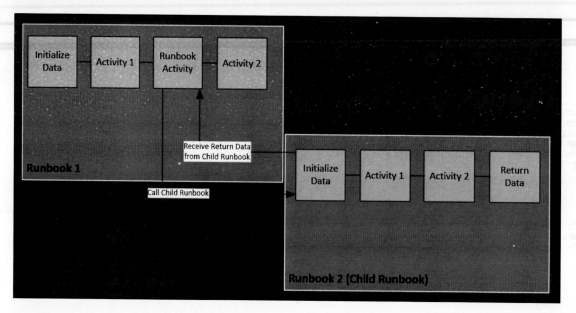

Getting ready

In our example, we will build a short user on-boarding with a Child Runbook to add the user in an Active Directory group. This child Runbook will be used multiple time, as our user needs to be in more than one group in our on-boarding process.

Perform the following steps in the Runbook Designer to prepare for the activity steps in this recipe:

1. In the Runbook Designer, expand the connection to the SCO 2016 server.
2. Navigate to our created Cookbook folder.
3. Right-click on folder 0.1-Cookbook and click on **New | Folder**.
4. Name the new folder 1.2-Chapter 4.

5. Also create the following folder Structure as you see in the screenshot here:

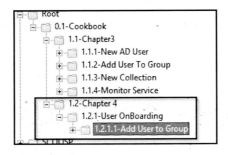

How to do it...

First, we will start building our child Runbook with *Add user to group*. Also, as simple add user to group can also be something more complex, we will also build a Runbook, which will solve this. Just think about what is happening when the user is already a member of this group, the Runbook would throw an error.

Follow the next steps to create our Runbook to add an Active Directory user to an Active Directory Group. A best practice is to start your activities from left to right in the design pane:

1. Create a Runbook with the name `1.2.1.1-Add User to Group` under the same folder.
2. Navigate to the **Activities** section in the Runbook Designer. Click on **Runbook Control**, and select and drag an **Initialize Data** activity to the middle pane of the Runbook (start from the leftmost part of the pane and work to the right as you add additional activities).
3. Right-click on **Initialize Data | Properties**. Click on **Add** two times, and use the following table to configure the three parameters in the **Details** section by clicking on each of the parameters in turn. Click on **Finish**:

Name of the parameter	Data type	Contains information
User SamAccountName	String	Will contain the SamAccountName of your user
Group SamAccountName	String	Will contain the SamAccountName of your group

4. Navigate to the **Activities** section. Click on **Active Directory**, and select and drag a **Get User** activity into the middle pane of the Runbook to the right of the **Initialize Data** object.

5. Link the **Initialize Data** and **Get User** activities (see Chapter 3, *Planning and Creating Runbook Designs, Understanding the Orchestrator Scenario Building Blocks* recipe, for information on linking activities):

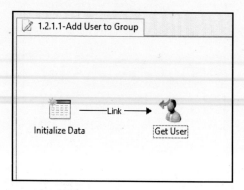

6. Double-click on the **Get User** activity and choose a connection to your Active Directory under Properties.

7. Next, navigate to the **Filters** section and configure like you see here:

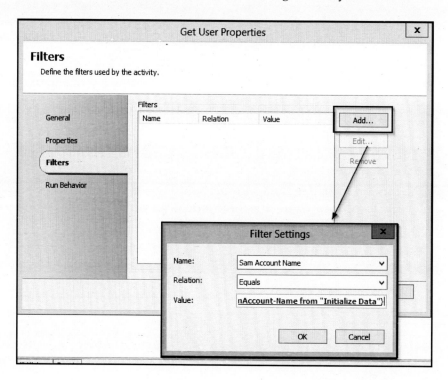

8. Navigate to the **Activities** section and click on **Active Directory**. Select and drag a **Get Group** activity in the middle pane of the Runbook next to the **Get User** activity.

9. Link the **Get User** activity to the **Get Group** activity:

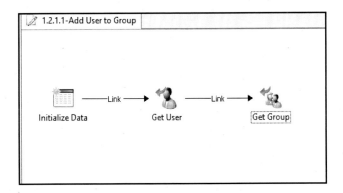

10. Double-click on the **Get Group** activity and choose a **Connection to your Active Directory** under **Properties**.

11. Next, navigate to the **Filters** section and configure as you see in the screenshot:

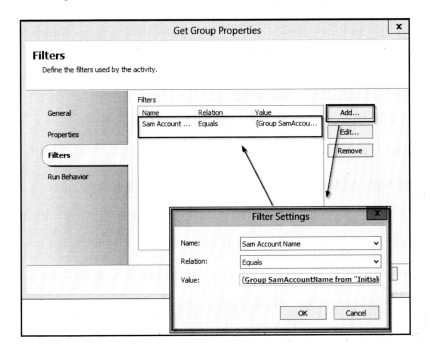

12. Stay at the **Filters** page; we need to configure one more filter:

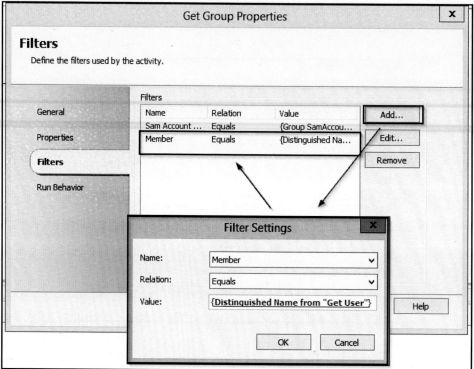

13. This will make sure that we can control whether the user is already in this group or not.

14. Navigate to the **Activities** section and click on **Active Directory**. Select and drag an **Add User to Group** activity in the middle pane of the Runbook next to the **Get Group** activity.

15. Link the **Get Group** activity to the **Add User to the Group** activity:

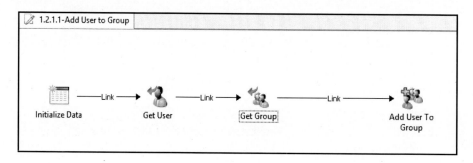

16. Double-click on the **Link** between **Get Group** activity and **Add User to Group** activity and configure the **Link**, as shown here:

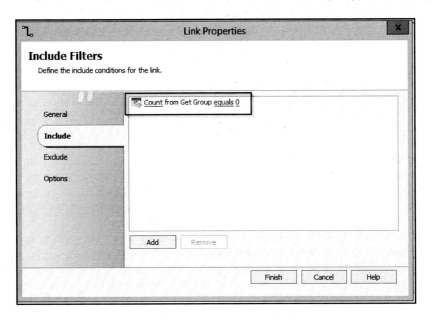

17. Last, navigate to **General** and name your link to make the Runbook easy and readable:

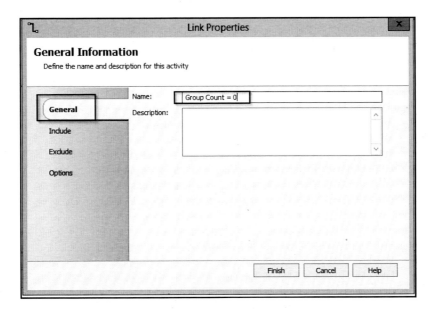

The final Runbook should look like this:

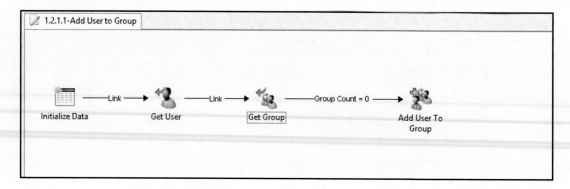

Now that our Child Runbook is finished, navigate to our `Runbook 1.1.1-New AD User` folder we created in `Chapter 3`, *Planning and Creating Runbook Designs*, to add the call for our child Runbook:

1. Navigate to the **Activities** section and click on **Runbook Control**. Select and drag a **Select Runbook** activity in the middle pane of Runbook next to the **Enable User** activity.

2. To drop the new activity between **Enable User** and **Append Line** activity, right-click on the **Link** between **Detach**, and attach it to the new **Invoke Runbook** activity:

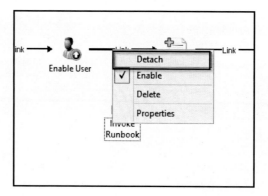

and set the link to the new Activity:

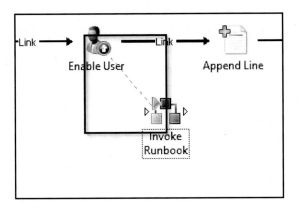

3. Now, link Runbook activity to **Append Line** activity and drag and drop the new activity to fit the Line:

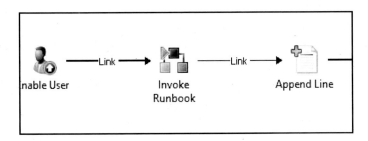

4. Double-click on the **Invoke Runbook** activity.

5. Click the ... icon and navigate to our `Add User to Group` Runbook and select this:

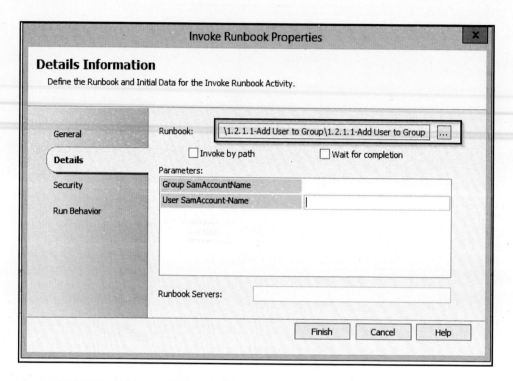

6. The **Initialized Data** from `1.2.1.1-Add User to Group` will show up; configure it like you see it in the screenshot:

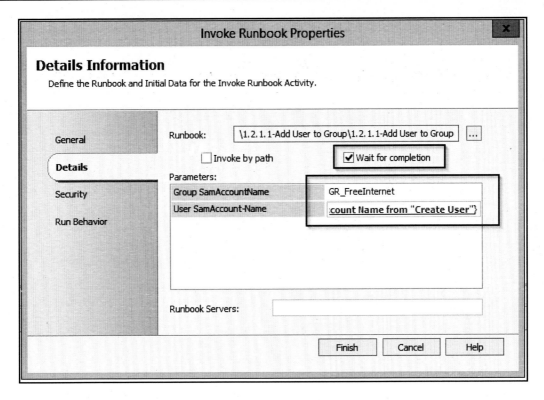

7. Now, the Runbook should look like this:

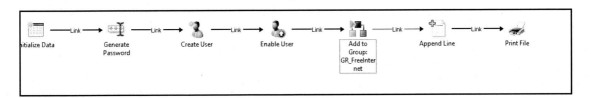

Repeat this steps for each group you would like to add the new user to.

How it works...

A child Runbook is used for Tasks that will be used by different Runbooks, and it is also useful to keep the master Runbook small and simple. So each step in a Runbook, which uses more than 1 activity, should be built in a separate child Runbook.

The configuration on the `Invoke Runbook` activity is important. As you saw in this chapter, there is the Option to **Wait form Completion**; this means that the master Runbook will call the next activity after the child Runbook is finished. This is very important when you receive some output from the child Runbook.

If your master Runbook does not depend to the child Runbook, you can uncheck this option, so your master Runbook will be much faster.

There's more...

The use of Variables is a key Feature in System Center 2016 Orchestrator. Save Information to a relate to the Variable from several Runbooks.

Using variables in different Runbook activities

Instead of manually typing the same text information each time, you can define variables for this in the Runbook Designer.

For instance, we need the group name for free internet a number of times in all the Runbooks. So, this group name can also be changed afterwards; if you use the **Variable**, just change the **Variable**, and all your Runbooks will use the new group name.

To add a variable follow these steps:

1. Expand the **Global Settings** | **Variables** section on the left-hand side of the Runbook Designer.
2. To organize your variables, you can add folders below the **Variables** section (this is optional but will aid with security delegation).
3. Create a new variable (right-click on **Variables** or a folder under **Variables** | **Variable**:

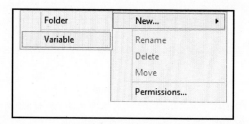

4. Fill in the information and click on **Finish**.

After this is done, you can use this variable in different Runbooks by selecting **Subscribe |
Variable**. Pick the variable you need from the available list of defined variables.

See also

Detailed information for the activities used in this Runbook can be found at Microsoft Docs
– Active Directory IP: `https://docs.microsoft.com/en-us/system-center/orchestrato
r/active-directory-activities`.

Building a looping Runbook

As a looping Runbook, we understand a Runbook contains an activity that loops until a
condition is met. As we have seen in our previous examples, each activity is running only
one time. A looping activity runs as much as the condition changes.

Getting ready

In this example, we will build a simple reboot Runbook where we restart a server and wait
until the server is going down and is coming up again, therefore we will need a looping
activity.

Perform the following steps in the Runbook Designer to prepare for the activity steps in this
recipe:

1. In the Runbook Designer, expand the connection to the SCO 2016 server.
2. Navigate to our created `1.2-Chapter 4` folder.
3. Create a new sub-folder called `1.2.2-Reboot a Server`:

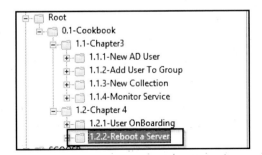

How to do it...

Follow the next steps to build a Reboot Runbook. Cause we are using the Initialize Data, your can use this Runbook to be called from other Runbooks, whenever you need to reboot a Server

1. Create a Runbook with the name `1.2.2-Reboot a Server` under the same named folder.

2. Navigate to the **Activities** section in the Runbook Designer. Click on **Runbook Control**, and select and drag an **Initialize Data** activity in the middle pane of the Runbook (start from the leftmost part of the pane and work to the right as you add additional activities).

3. Right-click on **Initialize Data | Properties**. Click on **Add** and use the following table to configure the parameter in the **Details** section by clicking on each of the parameters in turn. Click on **Finish**:

Name of the parameter	Data type	Contains information
Servername (FQDN)	String	Contains the Servername in FQDN format

4. Navigate to the **Activities** section in the Runbook Designer. Click on **System** and select and drag a **Restart System** activity to the middle pane of the Runbook.

5. Link the **Initialize Data** and **Restart System** activities (see Chapter 3, *Planning and Creating Runbook Designs, Understanding the Orchestrator Scenario Building Blocks* section, for information on linking activities).

6. Configure the **Restart System** activity as you see it in the following screenshot:

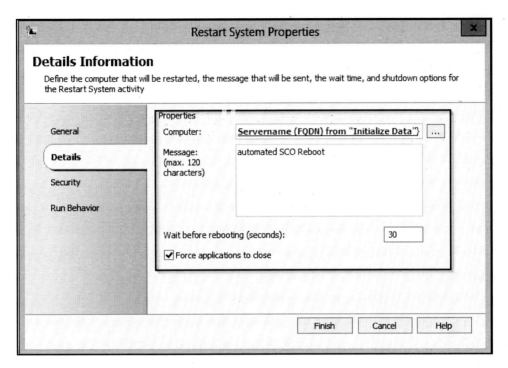

7. Navigate to the **Activities** section in the Runbook Designer. Click on **Monitoring** and select and drag an **Get Computer/IP Status** activity to the middle pane of the Runbook.

8. Link the **Restart System** and **Get Computer/IP Status** activities.

9. Configure the Activity as you see it in the screenshot:

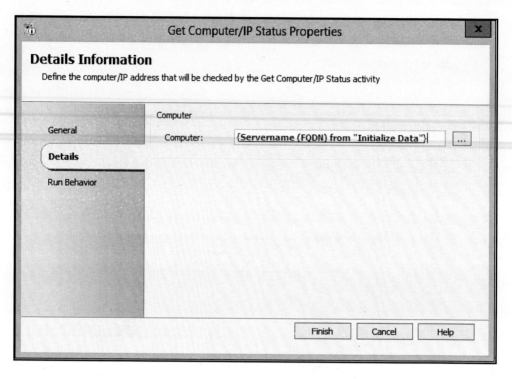

10. Also rename the activity to **Wait for Server Shutdown**.
11. Now right-click on **Wait for Server Shutdown** activity and select **Looping…**:

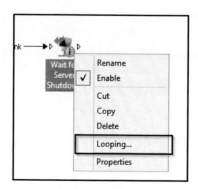

12. On the **General** tab please **Enable** Looping and enter 2 seconds as a **Delay between attempts**:

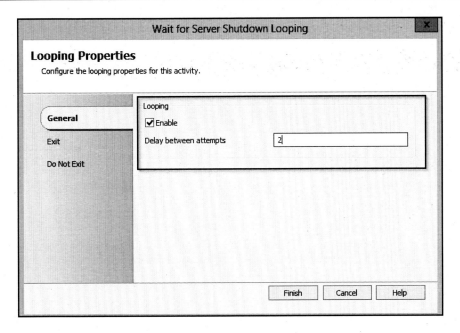

13. On the **Exit** tab, we need to configure the **Exit** conditions as you see it in the screenshot:

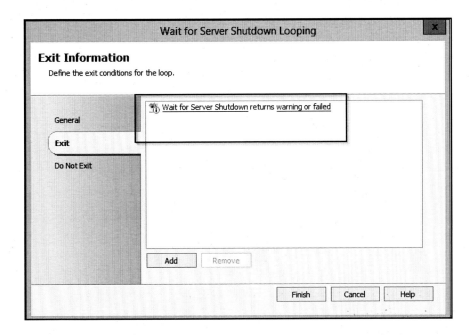

14. Now, click on **Finish** on this activity.

15. Navigate to the **Activities** section in the Runbook Designer. Click on **Monitoring** and select and drag an **Get Computer/IP Status** activity to the middle pane of the Runbook.

16. Link **Wait for Server Shutdown** and **Get Computer/IP Status** activities.

17. Configure the activity as you see in the screenshot:

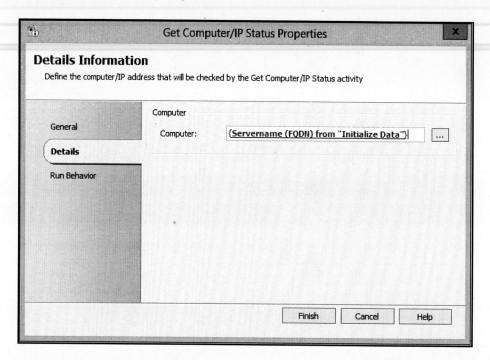

18. Also, rename the Activity to `Wait for Server Comeback`.

19. Now, right-click on **Wait for Server Comeback** activity and select **Looping....**

20. On the **General** tab, **Enable** Looping and enter 2 seconds as a **Delay between attempts**:

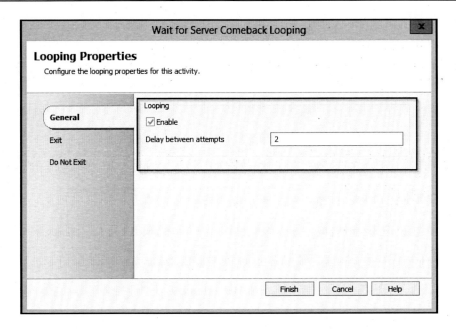

21. On the **Exit** tab, we need to configure the exit conditions as you see in the screenshot. Note, there are no changes to made, the default values are fine here:

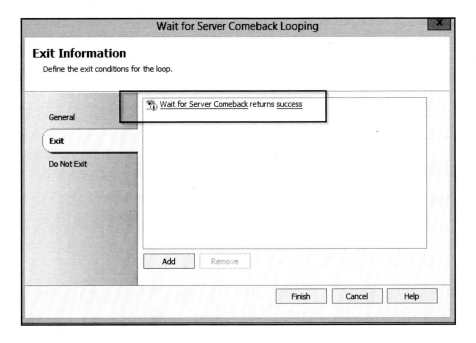

22. Double-click on the link between **Wait for Server Shutdown** activity and **Wait for Server Comeback** activity; and configure the link, as shown here:

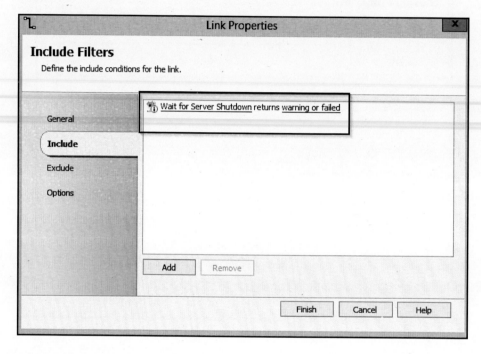

23. Also rename the Link to Return: warning or failed and change the color to orange.

24. The complete Runbook should look like this:

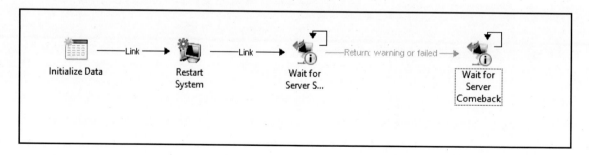

How it works…

For our Reboot Runbook, we took to use the **Get Computer/IP Status** activity. This activity will ping the configured computer and will return success if the computer has been contacted successfully. The activity will return a warning if the computer is not reachable.

So the **Wait for Server Shutdown** activity is doing a loop until the activity is running on a warning, because the computer wasn't reachable anymore.

The configuration of the link between those two loop activities is also important, because a default link is configured to fire when the previous activity is successful. In our Runbook, we are expecting a warning, so this was the reason why we have configured the link.

Also, always rename your Link and change the color when you are changing the default config, so your Runbook is much easier to read.

See also

Detailed information for the activities used in this Runbook can be found in *Implementing Error handling in your Runbooks* recipe, to enhance our Reboot Runbook and make sure there is no dead end.

For more information, refer to Microsoft TechNet – Get Computer/IP Status: `https://techn et.microsoft.com/en-us/library/hh206049(v=sc.12).aspx`.

Implementing logging in your Runbook

Until your Runbook is doing fine, logging is not often needed. But if there are problems, or maybe a case you didn't thought about during the initial Process of building your Runbooks, it is necessary to read some logs.

Getting ready

Runbooks already provide a log file, but only a very limited one with only less information about the start and end time and status; and if there is an error, the error message itself.

But this is not enough, so there should be a way to enhance the Logging of our Runbooks.

Navigate to your Runbook with the name `1.2.2-Reboot a Server`.

How to do it...

After the next Steps you will be able to activate enhanced Logging within your Runbooks, take care and only activate this for Debugging

1. Right-click on your Runbook and select **Properties**:

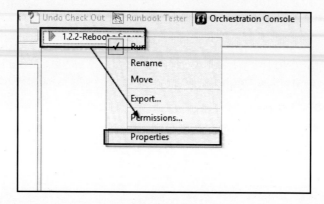

2. Navigate to the **Logging** tab:

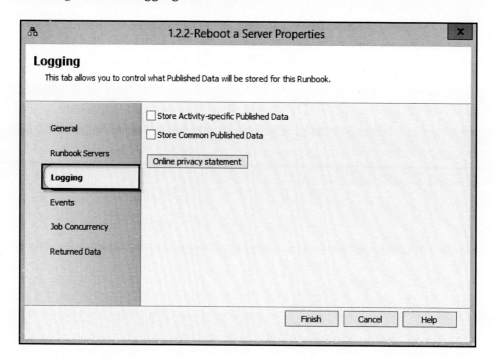

3. Select both options – **Store Activity-specific Published Data** and **Store Common Published Data**.

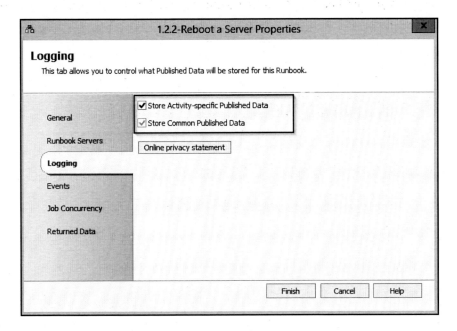

4. Save the **Properties** page by clicking on **OK** and check in your Runbook.

How it works...

To see how the enhanced logging is working, we will compare one Runbook and the logging information with both the types of logging.

In this example, you are seeing 2 logs: one is simple logging and one is the enhanced logging; you will not see any difference here:

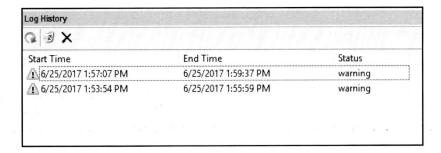

Simple logging

On double-clicking a log entry with simple logging mode, you will see all the activities within this Runbook each time they have been fired up:

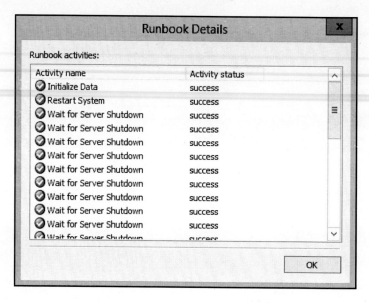

When you do a double-click on one of the activity, you will see the log of this activity, for example, double-click the **Initialize Data** activity:

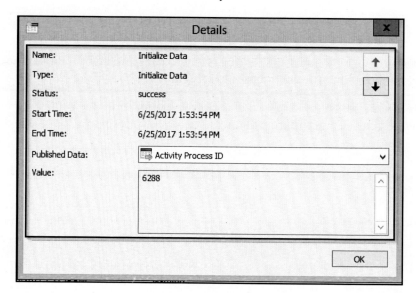

Here, you will see all the necessary things related to your activity; also see the navigation button on the top left, where you will be able to switch to the next activity.

On the drop-down menu, you can select whichever value you would like to see:

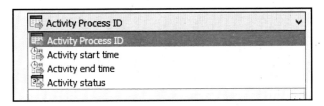

As you can see, there is nothing more on the **Details** before so that are all information's logged in the simple mode.

Enhanced logging

We have chosen a **Details** pane on an **Enhanced Logging** Runbook and selected the **Initialize Data** activity:

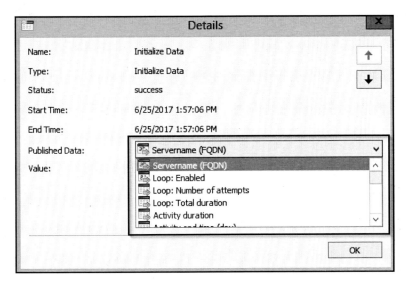

As you will see, there are a lot more values in the Enhanced Logging, so it will be much easier to troubleshoot with this much information:

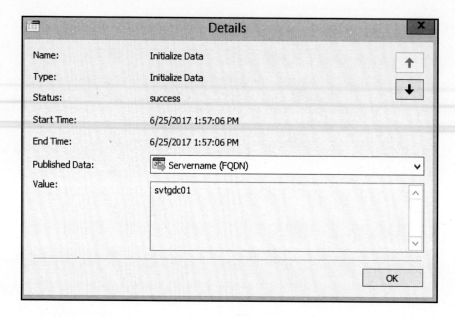

There is more...

As useful enhanced Logging will be, also think twice if you want to enabled this on your Runbooks.

Enhanced Logging will consume more process time and, of course, a lot more space in your SQL database to store all this information.

So, Enhanced Logging should only be used for testing and troubleshooting. Disable Enhanced Logging after your Runbook is finished and ready. Otherwise, your database will grow and your Orchestrator Environment can be unstable.

If you want to have more information in your Runbook for debugging or anything else, think about adding the **Append Line** activity and store all the information in a TXT File. This file can be easily moved to a different store and your SCO databases will stay small and fast.

Implementing error handling in your Runbooks

Always think about all the possible errors or problems, which can occur in your Runbooks, and try to build your Runbooks without a dead end.

There is nothing more annoying than a Runbook that seems to finish without any problem but is not doing what you are expecting because you have missed some possible ways, the Runbook can follow.

Getting ready

In our recipe, we will take care of our 1.2.2-Reboot a Server runbook and add some error handling. In case a server will stuck on the reboot process, our Runbook would wait endless time for the server to come back, so this is definitely not what we want; let's do this better in this recipe.

Navigate to your Runbook with the name 1.2.2-Reboot a Server.

How to do it...

After the following steps, you will be able to add Error Handling in your Runbooks:

1. Navigate to the **Activities** section in the Runbook Designer. Click on **Notification**; and select and drag an **Send Event Log Message** activity to the middle pane of the Runbook.
2. Link the **Wait for Server Shutdown** and **Send Event Log Message** activities.

3. Double-click on the **Send Event Log Message** activity and configure as you see in the screenshot:

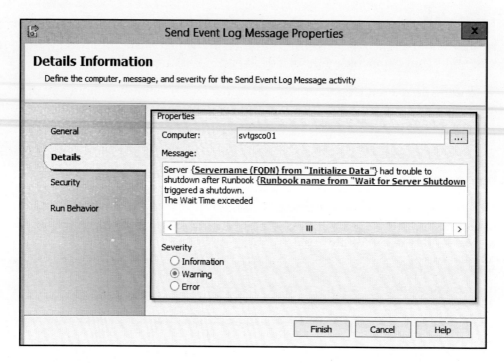

4. Now, right-click on **Wait for Server Shutdown** and select **Looping...**:

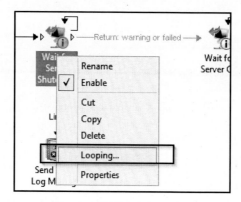

Navigate to the **Exit** tab, and click on **Add** to add a second condition to exit the Looping:

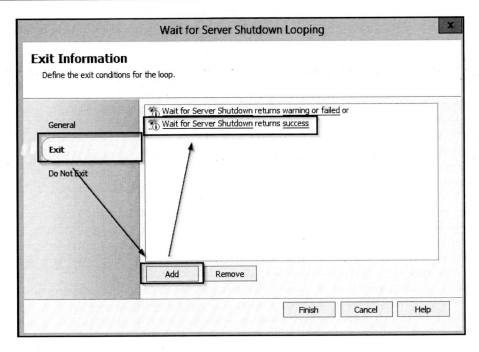

5. Next, click on the new line **Wait for Server Shutdown returns success**.

6. Enable **Show common Published Data** and Select **Loop: Number of attempts**:

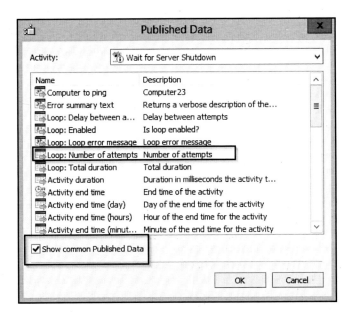

7. To complete the Condition, select **is greater than** and type the Value 150:

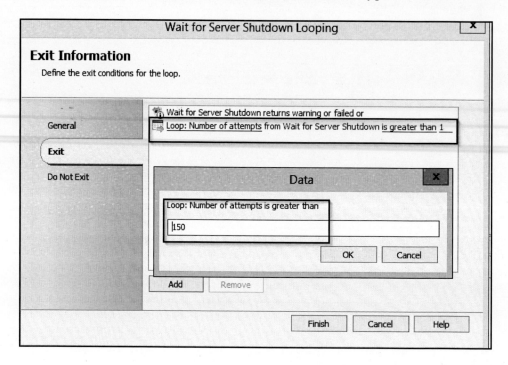

8. Double-click on the link between **Wait for Server Shutdown** and **Send Event Log Message**.

9. Change the condition to look like this:

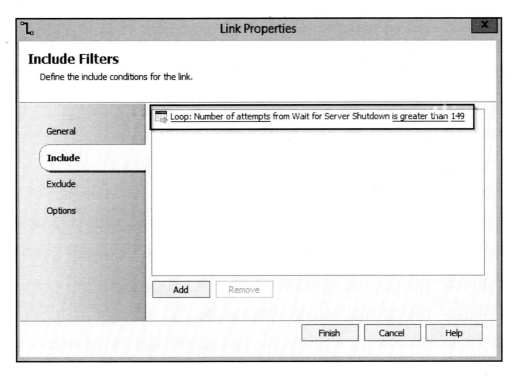

10. Navigate to the **Activities** section in the Runbook Designer. Click on **Notification**, and select and drag an **Send Event Log Message** activity to the middle pane of the Runbook.

11. Link the **Wait for Server Comeback** and **Send Event Log Message** activities.

12. Double-click on the **Send Event Log Message** activity and configure as you see here:

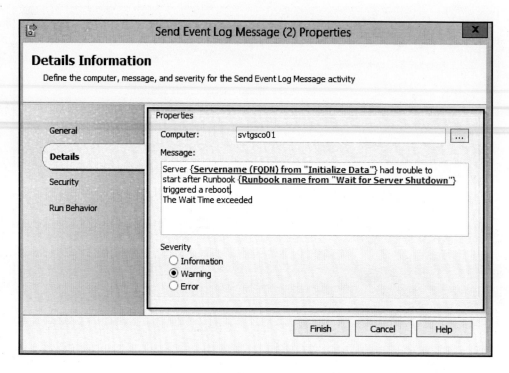

13. Now, right-click on **Wait for Server Comeback** and select **Looping...**:

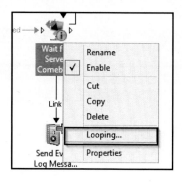

Navigate to the **Exit** tab, and click on **Add** to add a second condition to exit the **Looping...**:

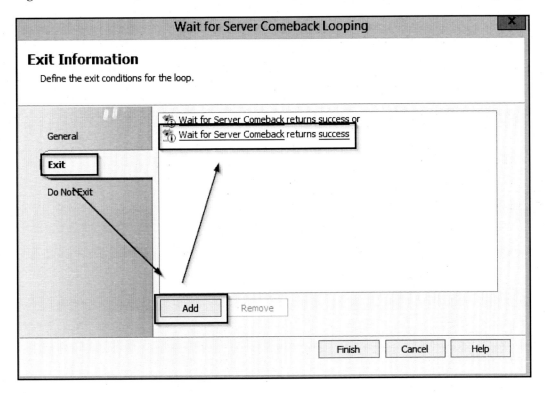

14. Next, click on the new line **Wait for Server Comeback returns success**.

15. Enable **Show common Published Data** and Select **Loop: Number of attempts**:

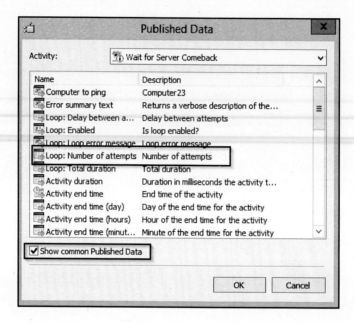

16. To complete the condition, select **is greater than** and type the value 150:

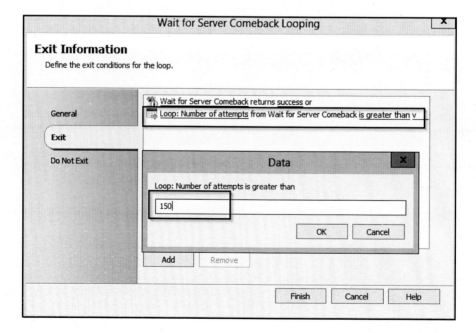

17. Double-click on the link between **Wait for Server Comeback** and **Send Event Log Message**.

18. Change the condition to look like this:

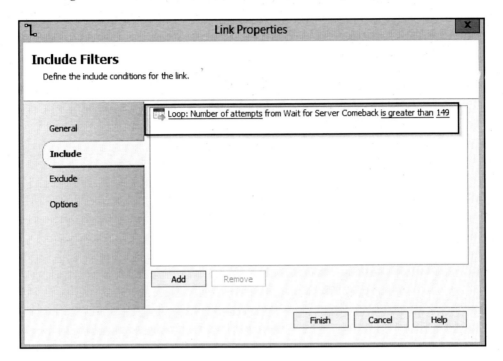

19. Check-in your Runbook.

How it works...

As you have seen in `Chapter 3`, *Planning and Creating Runbook Designs*, *Understanding the Orchestrator Scenario Building Blocks*, link filters are very important to control the flow of your Runbook.

We have configured the Looping Runbook to exit when it took more than 150 Attempts, so with 2 Seconds per Attempt, it will Time Out in 5 Minutes and will send an Event Log Message to our Runbook server.

You can also use a Send Mail activity or build a Child runbook for this Type of Alerting, but in the end, it is important to take make sure your Runbook will never ever have a dead end.

Making your Runbooks highly available

The default installation of System Center 2016 Orchestrator with multiple Runbook Servers automatically provides Runbook Server fault tolerance. The Runbooks you create will automatically run on an available Runbook Server if one of the multiple servers is unavailable. You have the option to control which Runbook Server a Runbook selects.

Getting ready

You must have a fully deployed SCO environment with two or more Runbook Servers in order to successfully complete the tasks in this recipe.

The planning criteria for this recipe is as detailed in the following table:

Runbook	Priority	Runbook Server availability
SLA 1 Runbook	High	All
SLA 5 Runbook	Low	1

How to do it...

Lets see what makes the difference between high priority Runbooks and low priority Runbooks.

High priority Runbook available on all Runbook Servers

Here you will see how to make sure that your Runbook will be executed on every available Runbook Server:

1. Log in to a SCO Runbook Designer computer with a user account with SCO administrative rights to the Runbooks in scope.
2. In the middle pane of the Runbook Designer, right-click on the Runbook in scope and select **Properties**. Click on the **Runbook Servers** tab.

3. Review **Override default Runbook Servers roles**. This setting must be unchecked to ensure the Runbook runs on a standby Runbook Server if the primary is unavailable:

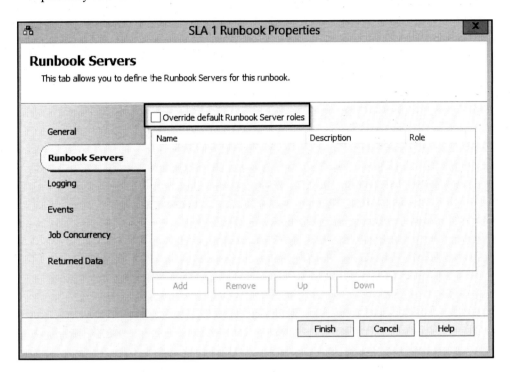

Low priority Runbook is available on one Runbook Server

Here you will see how to limit a Runbook to a single Runbook Server:

1. Log in to an SCO Runbook Designer computer with a user account with SCORCH administrative rights to the Runbooks in scope.

2. In the middle pane of the Runbook Designer, right-click on the Runbook in scope and select **Properties**. Select the **Runbook Servers** tab. Check **Override default Runbook Servers roles**. Click on **Add**:

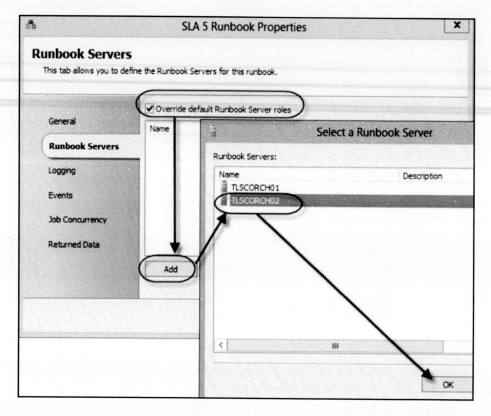

3. Click on **OK**. Click on **Finish** to complete the configuration. If prompted, select **Yes** to check out the Runbook.

How it works...

The default option in the first scenario is the standard for ensuring that SCO automatically manages the availability of Runbook Servers. In the case of the default, you are assured that your Runbook will be executed as long as at least one of the configured Runbooks is available.

The second option is useful for low priority Runbooks where you might want to control and limit the available Runbook Servers. It is recommended to leave the default setting for your premium Runbooks.

It might be beneficial to nominate a Runbook Server for testing purposes, and in this case, overriding the default setting may be a good option.

There's more...

You have the option to control the nominated primary Runbook Server setting globally for all Runbooks.

Promoting and demoting primary Runbook Servers

The first Runbook Server you install is nominated as the primary Runbook Server for all Runbooks by default. If you add additional Runbook Servers, you can also change the primary globally by following these steps:

1. Log in to an SCO Runbook Designer computer with a user account with SCORCH administrative rights to the Runbooks in scope.
2. Select **Runbook Servers** in the middle pane of the Runbook Designer. Right-click on the Runbook Server in scope and select **Promote to Primary**, **Promote**, or **Demote** to change the default system setting.

5
Simple Runbooks for Your Daily Tasks

In this chapter, we will be providing recipes on how to build simple Runbooks to automate your daily tasks

- Active Directory – Deleting inactive computer accounts
- SCOM – Activating maintenance mode for a server
- SCVMM – Removing an attached ISO from a VM
- SCCM – Automating the update installation process
- SCSM – Raising priority, if an affected user is a VIP

Introduction

Now that you are ready to use all the things you have learned in the last chapters, let's build some simple Runbooks, which will help in your daily business.

Active Directory – Deleting inactive computer accounts

You can schedule a Runbook in System Center 2016 Orchestrator to automatically remove disabled and obsolete computer accounts from Active Directory.

The business process of this workflow is defined in the following diagram:

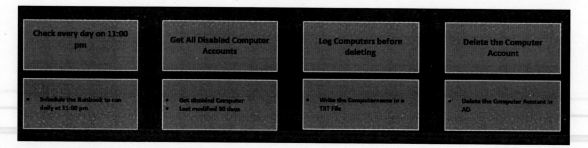

Getting ready

To get ready for our first Runbook., we need to create a new folder and a new Runbook in the Runbook Designer:

1. In the Runbook Designer, expand the connection to the SCO 2016 server.
2. Navigate to `Root\0.1-Cookbook`, and create a new folder called `1.3-Chapter 5`.
3. Create a subfolder called `1.3.1-Delete inactive Computer Accounts`.
4. Right-click on the new folder. and then click on **New** and select **Runbook**.
5. Right-click on the newly created Runbook, and rename it to `1.3.1-Delete inactive Computer Accounts`.

How to do it...

This Runbook requires a schedule, which is the first activity we need in our Runbook:

1. In the newly created Runbook, navigate to and click on **Scheduling** under **Activities**, and then select and drag a **Monitor Date/Time** activity into the middle pane of the Runbook:

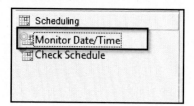

2. Double-click on the **Monitor Date/Time** activity. Configure the interval on the **Details** section using the information in the following table:

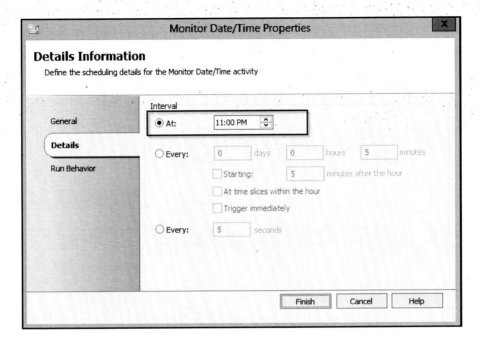

3. Click on **Finish**.
4. Navigate to the **Activities** section, and click on **Active Directory**; select and drag a **Get Computer** activity into the middle pane of the Runbook next to the **Monitor Date/Time** activity:

5. Link the **Monitor Date/Time** activity to the **Get Computer** activity.

6. Double-click on the **Get Computer** activity, and choose a connection to your Active Directory under **Properties**.

7. Next navigate to the **Filters** section and configure it as you see in the following screenshot:

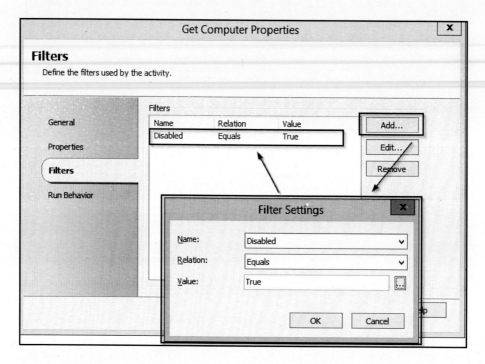

8. Click on **Finish**.

9. Navigate to the **Activities** section and click on **Utilities**. Select and drag a **Format Date/Time Modification Date** activity into the Runbook next to the **Get Computer** activity.

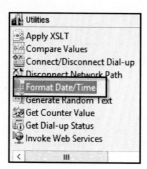

10. Link the **Get Computer** activity to the **Format Date/Time Modification Date** activity.

11. Double-click on the **Format Date/Time Modification Date** activity and provide the information shown. Right-click in the space next to **Date/Time** and select **Subscribe | Published Data | Get Computer | Modification Date**. Type dd/MM/yyyy hh:mm:ss in the **Format:** field under the **Output** section. Click on **Finish**.

12. Navigate to the **Activities** section, click on **System**, and drag a **Run .Net Script** activity into the middle pane of the Runbook next to the **Format Date/Time Modification Date** activity:

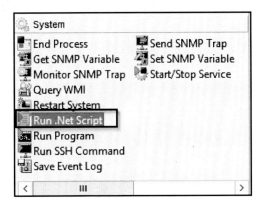

13. Link the **Format Date/Time Modification Date** activity to the **Run .Net Script** activity.

14. Rename the **Run .Net Script** activity to **PowerShell Script Compare Modification Date**.

15. Double-click on the **PowerShell Script Compare Modification Date** activity, and select **PowerShell** in the **Language | Type** field on the **Details** section (use the ... button to select).

16. Right-click on the **Script** field, and select **Expand** to open up the **Script** field. Add the code shown in the following screenshot into the **Script** field:

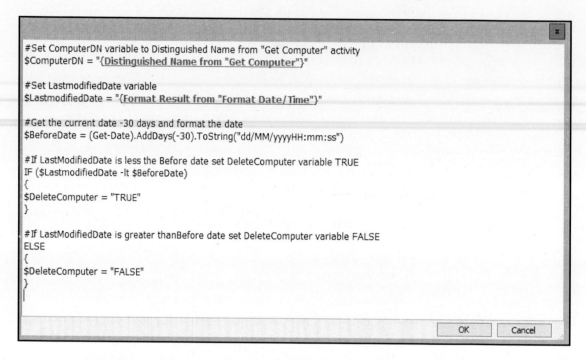

```
#Set ComputerDN variable to Distinguished Name from "Get Computer" activity
$ComputerDN = "{Distinguished Name from "Get Computer"}"

#Set LastmodifiedDate variable
$LastmodifiedDate = "{Format Result from "Format Date/Time"}"

#Get the current date -30 days and format the date
$BeforeDate = (Get-Date).AddDays(-30).ToString("dd/MM/yyyyHH:mm:ss")

#If LastModifiedDate is less the Before date set DeleteComputer variable TRUE
IF ($LastmodifiedDate -lt $BeforeDate)
{
$DeleteComputer = "TRUE"
}

#If LastModifiedDate is greater thanBefore date set DeleteComputer variable FALSE
ELSE
{
$DeleteComputer = "FALSE"
}
```

17. In the **PowerShell Script Compare Modification Date** activity, select the **Published Data** tab, and add the two properties with their respective values using the screenshot here (Click on **Finish** on completion):

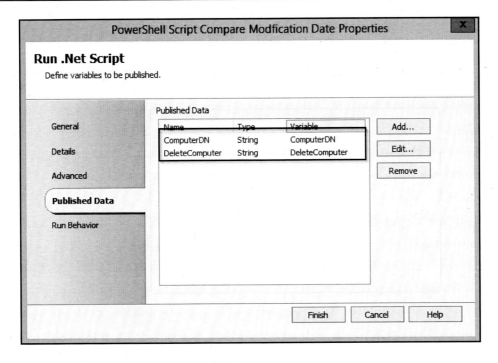

18. Click on **Finish**.
19. Navigate to the **Activities** section in the Runbook Designer. Click on **Text File Management** select, and drag an **Append Line** activity into the Runbook next to the **PowerShell Script Compare Modification Date**:

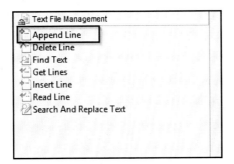

20. Link the **PowerShell Script Compare Modification Date** activity to the **Append Line** activity.

21. Double-click on the link (it is the arrowed line between the two activities), and modify the **Include Filter**. Double-click on the existing information in the **Include Filter** and select **DeleteUser**, click on **OK** and then on value. Type TRUE. Click on **OK** and then on **Finish**.

22. Double-click on the **Append Line** activity, and configure the activity with the information from the following Screenshot:

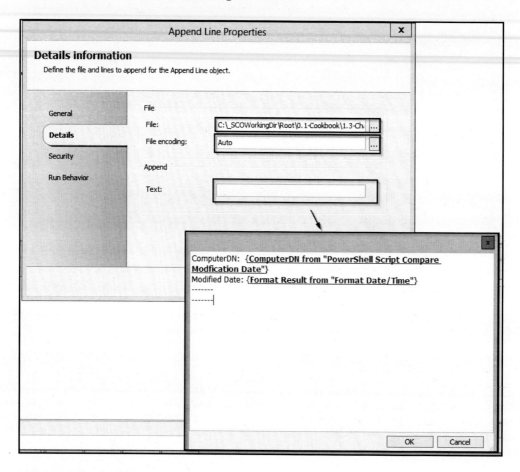

23. Click on **Finish**.

24. Navigate to the **Activities** section in the Runbook Designer; click on **Active Directory**. Select and drag a **Delete Computer** activity into the middle pane of the Runbook next to the **Append Line** activity:

25. Link the **Append Line** activity to the **Delete User** activity.

26. Double-click on the **Delete Computer** activity, and choose a connection to your Active Directory under **Properties**.

27. On the **Distinguished Name** property, select the **Published Date Distinguished Name** from the **Get Computer** Activity:

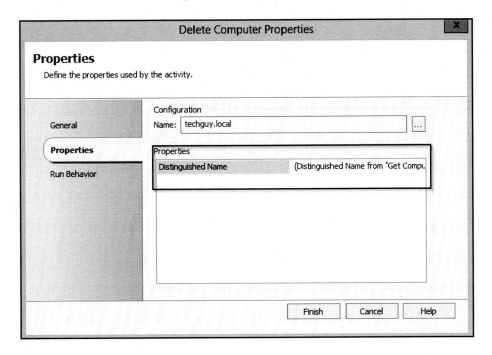

28. Click on **Finish**.

It is easy to use the Runbook Tester to test this Runbook. As a recommended best practice, you should plan to test this in a lab/development environment. The user accounts found by the **Get Computer** activity and filtered into the PowerShell script will be deleted even if the Runbook is run in the Runbook Tester! For testing in a production environment, it is a good idea to disable the link between the **Append Line** activity and the **Delete Computer** activity" (right-click on the link and deselect **Enabled**). This way the filtered users are logged in the text file but not deleted during the test.

The Runbook should look like this now:

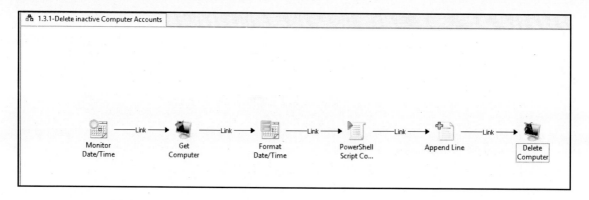

How it works...

This Runbook needs to be checked-in and started (run) to execute. Though the Runbook is running, the actions will only be executed at the time specified in the schedule. In this example, it will be started at 11:00 P.M. everyday (**Monitor Date/Time** activity).

In the **Get Computer** activity, the disabled computers will be queried from Active Directory. The modification date is formatted in the **Format Date/Time Modification Date** activity for the next step.

For each disabled computer discovered by the Active Directory query, the PowerShell Script will compare the formatted modification date against the current date—30 days before. See the comment lines in the script for details:

```
#Set ComputerDN variable to Distinguished Name from "Get Computer" activity
$ComputerDN = "{Distinguished Name from "GetComputer"}"
#Set LastmodifiedDate variable
$LastmodifiedDate = "{Format Result without adjustments from "Format
Date/Time Modification Date"}"
#Get the current date -30 days and format the date
$BeforeDate = (Get-Date).AddDays(-30).ToString("dd/MM/yyyyHH:mm:ss")
#If LastModifiedDate is less the Before date set DeleteComputer variable
TRUE
IF ($LastmodifiedDate -lt $BeforeDate)
{
$DeleteComputer = "TRUE"
}
#If LastModifiedDate is greater thanBefore date set DeleteComputer variable
FALSE
ELSE
{
$DeleteComputer = "FALSE"
}
```

If the DeleteComputer variable is equal to TRUE the distinguished name of the computer and the current date are logged in a text file (**Append Line** activity). If the DeleteComputer variable is FALSE, nothing will happen.

In the last activity, the disabled computer accounts, which were last modified 30 days ago, were deleted in Active Directory (**Delete Computer** activity).

There's more...

Deleting disabled computer is the safe way to cleanup your Active Directory. It would be possible to delete all computer with a **LastModified Date** older than XX days. Here make sure that XX is enough time to make sure you will not delete computers of user during holiday.

Deleting obsolete user accounts in Active Directory

To delete obsolete user accounts, you can use the activities **Get User** and **Delete User** of the Active Directory Integration Pack.

It is also possible to run a PowerShell script to get obsolete users or computers by their last logon time. But take care to get the last logon time from all your domain controllers, otherwise you accidentally delete a user or computer which is still active.

See also

Detailed information for the activities used in this Runbook you can find here:

- Microsoft Technet—Monitor Date/Time activity: `http://technet.microsoft.co m/en-us/library/hh225031.aspx`
- Microsoft Technet—Get Computer activity: `https://docs.microsoft.com/en-u s/system-center/orchestrator/get-computer`
- Microsoft Technet—Format Date/Time activity: `http://technet.microsoft.com /en-us/library/hh206037.aspx`
- Microsoft Technet—Run .Net Script activity: `http://technet.microsoft.com/e n-us/library/hh206103.aspx`
- Microsoft Technet—Append Line activity: `http://technet.microsoft.com/en- us/library/hh206072.aspx`
- Microsoft Technet—Delete Computer activity: `https://docs.microsoft.com/en -us/system-center/orchestrator/delete-computer`
- Microsoft Technet Gallery Download—Get Inactive Computer in Domain based on Last Logon Time Stamp: `https://gallery.technet.microsoft.com/Get-In active-Computer-in-54feafde`

SCOM – Activating maintenance mode for a server

The System Center Operations Manager Integration Pack for Orchestrator 2016 is limited to its activities. One of the most used task for SCOM will be to set a server in maintenance mode. This activity does exists, but is not really easy to use, so let's create a Runbook for it.

Getting ready

In this Runbook, we need to use some variables, so navigate to Global Settings\Variables\Root, and create two variables as you see in the following table:

Name	Description	Value
SCOM Service User Passwords	This contains the Service User Password	*****
SCOM Service User Usernames	This contains the Service User Username	*Domain**Username*
SCOM Servername s(FQDN)	This contains your SCOM Servername	*server.doamin.lcoal*

To get ready for our next Runbook, we need to create a new Folder and a new Runbook in the Runbook Designer:

1. In the Runbook Designer, expand the connection to the SCO 2016 server.
2. Navigate to Root\0.1-Cookbook\1.3-Chapter 5, and create a new folder called 1.3.2-Activate SCOM Maintenance Mode.

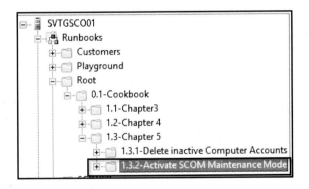

How to do it...

This Runbook will activate the SCOM Maintenance Mode for the server you put in the Initialize Data:

1. Right-click on the new folder, and then click on **New** and select **Runbook**.
2. Right-click on the newly created Runbook, and rename it to 1.3.2-Activate SCOM Maintenance Mode.

3. Navigate to the **Activities** section in the Runbook Designer. Click on **Runbook Control**, and select and drag an **Initialize Data** activity to the middle pane of the Runbook (start from the leftmost part of the pane and work to the right as you add additional activities).

4. Right-click on **Initialize Data | Properties**. Click on **Add** and use the following table to configure the parameter in the **Details** section by clicking on each of the parameters in turn. Click on **Finish**:

Name of parameter	Data type	Contains information
Servername (FQDN)	String	This contains the server name in FQDN format
Duration in Minutes	String	This contains the time in minutes as duration for the SCOM maintenance mode
Comment	String	This contains the comment as string

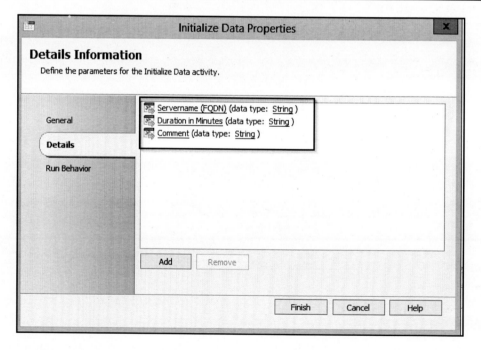

5. Click on **Finish**.

6. Navigate to the **Activities** section, click on **System** and drag a **Run .Net Script** activity into the middle pane of the Runbook next to the **Initialize Data** activity:

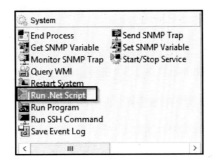

7. Link the **Initialize Data** activity to the **Run .Net Script** activity.

8. Rename the **Run .Net Script** activity to **Start Maintenance Mode**.

9. Double-click on the **Start Maintenance Mode** activity, and select PowerShell in the **Language** | **Type** field on the **Details** section (use the **...** button to select).

10. Right-click on the **Script** field and select **Expand** to open up the **Script** field. Add the code shown in the following screenshot into the **Script** field:

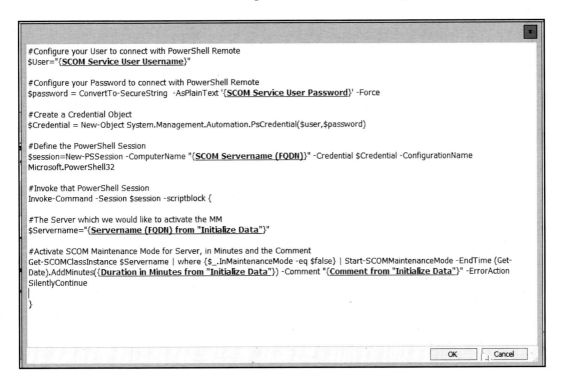

```
#Configure your User to connect with PowerShell Remote
$User="{SCOM Service User Username}"

#Configure your Password to connect with PowerShell Remote
$password = ConvertTo-SecureString  -AsPlainText '{SCOM Service User Password}' -Force

#Create a Credential Object
$Credential = New-Object System.Management.Automation.PsCredential($user,$password)

#Define the PowerShell Session
$session=New-PSSession -ComputerName "{SCOM Servername (FQDN)}" -Credential $Credential -ConfigurationName
Microsoft.PowerShell32

#Invoke that PowerShell Session
Invoke-Command -Session $session -scriptblock {

#The Server which we would like to activate the MM
$Servername="{Servername (FQDN) from "Initialize Data"}"

#Activate SCOM Maintenance Mode for Server, in Minutes and the Comment
Get-SCOMClassInstance $Servername | where {$_.InMaintenanceMode -eq $false} | Start-SCOMMaintenanceMode -EndTime (Get-
Date).AddMinutes({Duration in Minutes from "Initialize Data"}) -Comment "{Comment from "Initialize Data"}" -ErrorAction
SilentlyContinue

}
```

The Runbook should look like this now:

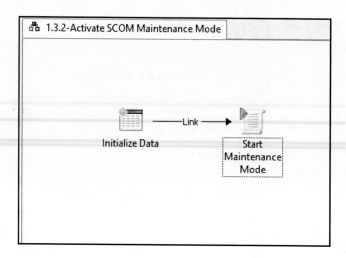

How it works...

The entered server name will be passed to the to **Start Maintenance Mode** activity. Also the comment and the minutes will be used from the **Initialize Data** activity:

```
#Configure your User to connect with PowerShell Remote
$User="{SCOM Service User Username}"

#Configure your Password to connect with PowerShell Remote
$password = ConvertTo-SecureString  -AsPlainText '{SCOM Service User
Password}' -Force

#Create a Credential Object
$Credential = New-Object
System.Management.Automation.PsCredential($user,$password)

#Define the PowerShell Session
$session=New-PSSession -ComputerName "SCOM Servername (FQDN)" -Credential
$Credential -ConfigurationName Microsoft.PowerShell32

#Invoke that PowerShell Session
Invoke-Command -Session $session -scriptblock {

#The Server which we would like to activate the MM
$Servername="{Servername (FQDN) from "Initialize Data"}"

#Activate SCOM Maintenance Mode for Server, in Minutes and the Comment
```

```
Get-SCOMClassInstance $Servername | where {$_.InMaintenanceMode -eq $false}
| Start-SCOMMaintenanceMode -EndTime (Get-Date).AddMinutes({Duration in
Minutes from "Initialize Data"}) -Comment "{Comment from "Initialize
Data"}" -ErrorAction SilentlyContinue

}
```

The PowerShell Script will connect with a PowerShell remote session to the SCOM server, and it will call the SCOM PowerShell cmdlet to activate the maintenance mode.

There's more...

In this recipe, you have seen how to activate the SCOM maintenance mode for a defined period of time.

But it is also possible to create a Runbook to stop the maintenance mode; for this, just follow these steps:

1. In the Runbook Designer, expand the connection to the SCO 2016 server.
2. Navigate to `Root\0.1-Cookbook\1.3-Chapter 5`, and create a new folder called `1.3.3-Stop SCOM Maintenance Mode`.
3. Right-click on the new folder, and then click on **New** and select **Runbook**.
4. Right-click on the newly created Runbook, and rename it to `1.3.3-Stop SCOM Maintenance Mode`.
5. Navigate to the **Activities** section in the Runbook Designer. Click on **Runbook Control**, and select and drag an **Initialize Dat**a activity to the middle pane of the Runbook (start from the leftmost part of the pane and work to the right as you add additional activities).

6. Right-click on **Initialize Data** | **Properties**. Click on **Add**, and use the following table to configure the parameter in the **Details** section by clicking on each of the parameters in turn. Click on **Finish**:

Name of parameter	Data type	Contains information
Servername (FQDN)	**String**	This contains the server name in FQDN format

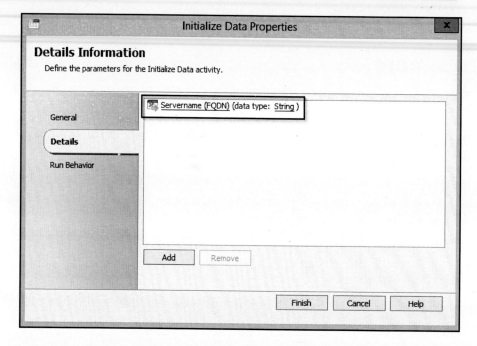

7. Navigate to the **Activities** section, click on **System**, and drag a **Run .Net Script** activity into the middle pane of the Runbook next to the **Initialize Data** activity:

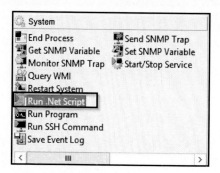

8. Link the **Initialize Data** activity to the **Run .Net Script** activity.

9. Rename the **Run .Net Script** activity to **Stop Maintenance Mode**.

10. Double-click on the `Stop Maintenance Mode` activity, and select **PowerShell** in the **Language | Type** field in the **Details** section (use the **...** button to select).

11. Right-click on the **Script** field and select **Expand** to open up the **Script** field. Add the code shown in the following screenshot into the **Script** field:

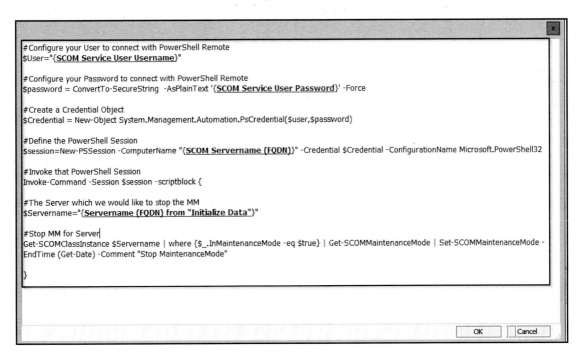

```
#Configure your User to connect with PowerShell Remote
$User="{SCOM Service User Username}"

#Configure your Password to connect with PowerShell Remote
$password = ConvertTo-SecureString  -AsPlainText '{SCOM Service User Password}' -Force

#Create a Credential Object
$Credential = New-Object System.Management.Automation.PsCredential($user,$password)

#Define the PowerShell Session
$session=New-PSSession -ComputerName "{SCOM Servername (FQDN)}" -Credential $Credential -ConfigurationName Microsoft.PowerShell32

#Invoke that PowerShell Session
Invoke-Command -Session $session -scriptblock {

#The Server which we would like to stop the MM
$Servername="{Servername (FQDN) from "Initialize Data"}"

#Stop MM for Server
Get-SCOMClassInstance $Servername | where {$_.InMaintenanceMode -eq $true} | Get-SCOMMaintenanceMode | Set-SCOMMaintenanceMode -EndTime (Get-Date) -Comment "Stop MaintenanceMode"

}
```

The Runbook should look like this now:

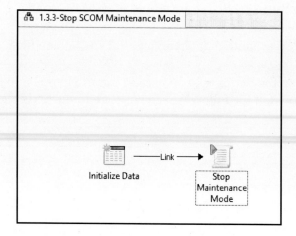

See also

Detailed information for the activities used in this Runbook can be found at Microsoft Technet—Run .Net Script activity at `http://technet.microsoft.com/en-us/library/hh 206103.aspx`.

SCVMM – Removing an attached ISO from a VM

The recommended current practice for clustered Hyper-V host maintenance is to live migrate all VMs on the target host to a different host. This practice also applies if you utilize the SCVMM host migration features of dynamic and power optimization.

Live migration and dynamic and power optimization will normally happen successfully in the background. Any VMs with ISO images attached during either of these tasks will not successfully migrate. The result of a failed migration in either case is possible downtime or degraded performance.

This recipe will show you how to automate the location and removal of attached ISO images on a predefined schedule.

Getting ready

This recipe will leverage System Center 2016 Virtual Machine Manager to find and remediate all the VMs with mounted ISO Images.

To successfully finish this recipe, follow the recipes in `Chapter 2`, *The Initial Configuration of SCO 2016*, to register, deploy, and configure the SCVMM Integration Pack.

You will need to mount an ISO image to at least one VM for testing:

1. In the Runbook Designer, expand the connection to the SCO 2016 server.
2. Navigate to `Root\0.1-Cookbook\1.3-Chapter 5`, and create a new folder called `1.3.4-Remove attached ISO from VM`.

How to do it...

The following steps will show you how to configure the activities to create the Runbook for this recipe:

1. Right-click on the new folder, and then click on **New** and select **Runbook**.
2. Right-click on the newly created Runbook, and rename it to `1.3.4-Remove attached ISO from VM`.
3. Navigate to the **Activities** section in the Runbook Designer, select **Scheduling**, and drag a **Monitor Date/Time** activity into the middle pane of the Runbook (the workspace).
4. Right-click on the activity and choose **Rename**. Rename the activity to **Start at 09:30 PM**.
5. Right-click on the activity and choose **Properties**.
6. Change the **Interval** to `At: 09:30 PM`, and click on **Finish**.

7. Navigate to the **Activities** section, select **SC 2016 Virtual Machine Manager**, and drag a **Get VM** activity into the Runbook next to the **Start at 21:30** activity:

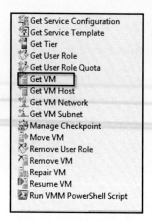

8. Link the **Start at 21:30** activity to the **Get VM** activity.
9. Double-click on the **Get VM** activity, and choose a connection to your SCVMM under **Properties**.
10. Click on **Finish**.
11. Navigate to the **Activities** section, select **SC 2016 Virtual Machine Manager**, and drag a **Run VMM PowerShell Script** activity to the Runbook next to the **Get VM** object:

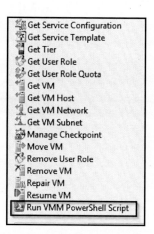

12. Link the **Get VM** activity to the **Run VMM PowerShell Script** activity.
13. Right-click on the **Run VMM PowerShell Script**, and choose **Rename**.

14. Rename the activity to **Find VMs with ISO Attached**.
15. Double-click on the **Find VMs with ISO Attached** activity and provide the following information:

Name of parameter	Value
Configuration name	Pick the SCVMM configuration you set up in the preparation of this chapter from the list.

PowerShell script	`$VM = '{VM Name from "Get VM"}'`
	`$ISO = get-scvirtualdvddrive -VM $VM`
	`$HasISO = $ISO.ISOLinked`
	Replace {VM Name from "Get VM"} by right-clicking on the **PowerShell Script** field and navigate to **Subscribe | Published Data**. Choose **Get VM** in the **Activity** field and select **VM Name**.

Output variable 1	`$HasISO`

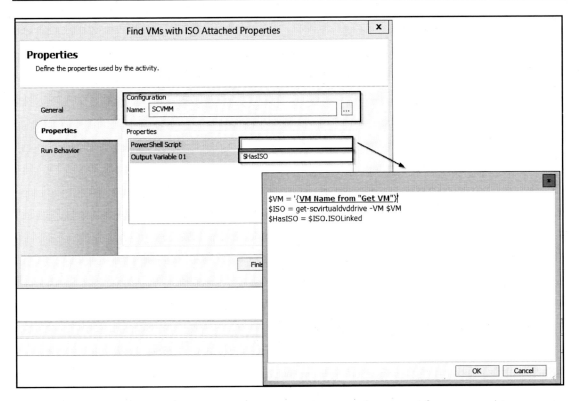

16. Click on **Finish**.

17. Navigate to the **Activities** section, select **SC 2016 Virtual Machine Manager**, and drag the **Run VMM PowerShell Script** activity to the Runbook next to the **Find VMs with ISO Attached** object.

18. Link the **Find VMs with ISO Attached** activity to the **Run VMM PowerShell Script** activity.

19. Right-click on the **Run VMM PowerShell Script** and select **Rename**.

20. Rename the activity to Remove ISO.

21. Double-click on the link between the **Find VMs with ISO Attached and Remove ISO** activities.

22. Click on the **Find VMs with ISO Attached** text.

23. Select **Output Variable 01** from the list, and click on **OK**.

24. Click the underlined text value.

25. Type True and click on **OK**:

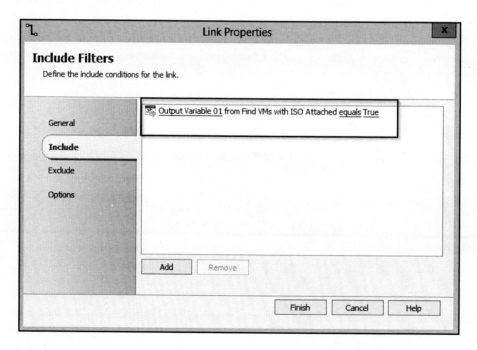

26. Click on **Finish**.

27. Double-click on the **Remove ISO** activity and provide the following information:

The name of parameter	Value
The Configuration name	Pick the SCVMM configuration we set up in the preparation of this chapter from the list.

The powerShell script	`$VM = '{VM Name from "Get VM"}'`
	`$ISO = Get-SCVirtualDVDDrive -VM $VM`
	`$UnMount = Set-SCVirtualDVDDrive -VirtualDVDDrive $ISO`
	`-NoMedia`
	`$IsISOLinked = $UnMount.ISOLinked`
	Replace {VM Name from "Get VM"} by right-clicking on the **PowerShell Script** field and navigate to **Subscribe | Published Data**. Choose **Get VM** in the **Activity** field and select **VM Name**.

Output variable 1	`$IsISOLinked`

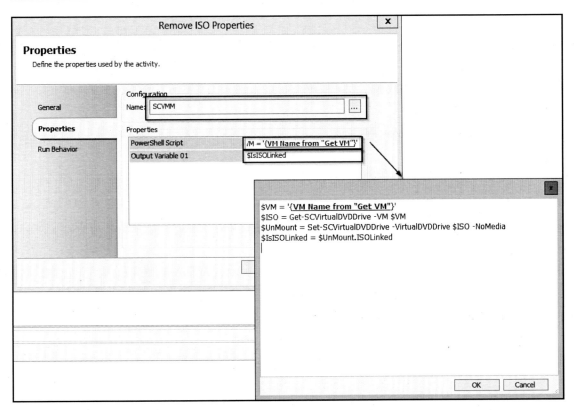

28. Click on **Finish**.
29. Navigate to the **Activities** section, select **Notification**, and drag a **Send Platform Event** activity to the Runbook next to the **Remove ISO** activity:

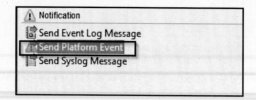

30. Right-click on the **Send Platform Event** and select **Rename**.
31. Rename the activity to **Log Removal**.
32. Link the **Remove ISO** activity to the **Log Removal** activity.
33. Double-click on the link between **Remove ISO** and **Log Removal** activities.
34. Click on the **Remove ISO** text.
35. Select **Output Variable 01** from the list, and click on **OK**.
36. Click the underlined word value.
37. Type `False` and click on **OK**.

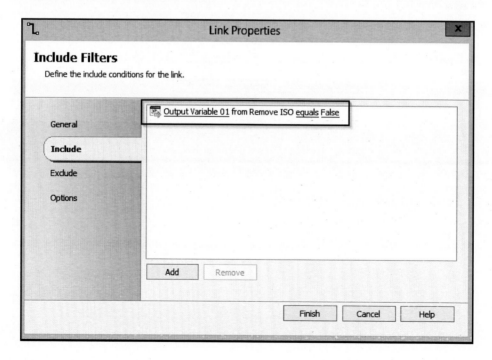

38. Click on **Finish**.
39. Click on the **Options** tab and change the **Color** to green:

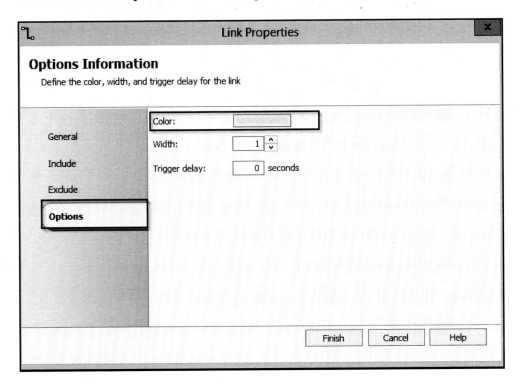

40. Click on **Finish**.
41. Double-click on the **Log Removal** activity and provide the following information in the **Details** section:

Name of parameter	Value
Type	Information
Summary	Type the following text: `Removed ISO Image`
Details	• Type the following text: `Removed ISO Image from.` • Then, right-click on the space after the word `from` and navigate to **Subscribe	Published Data**. • Choose **Get VM** in the **Activity** field and select **VM Name**.

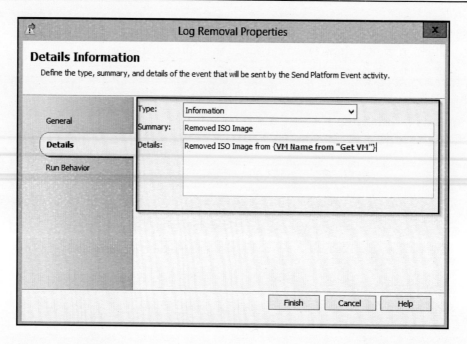

42. Click on **Finish**.
43. Navigate to the **Activities** section, select **Notification**. and drag the **Send Platform Event** activity to the Runbook below the **Remove ISO** activity.
44. Right-click on the **Send Platform Event** activity, and select **Rename**.
45. Rename the activity to `Log Failure`.
46. Link the **Remove ISO** activity to the **Log Failure** activity.
47. Double-click on the link between the **Remove ISO** and **Log Failure** activities.
48. Click on the word **success** next to the **Remove ISO returns** text.

49. Uncheck **success** and check **failed**, and then click on **OK**.

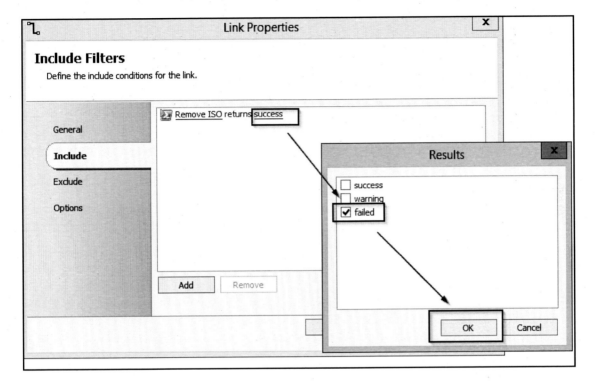

50. Click on **Finish**.
51. Click on **Add**, then click on the **Remove ISO** text.
52. Choose **Output Variable 01** from the list, and click on **OK**.

53. Click the underlined word value.
54. Type `True` and click on **OK**.

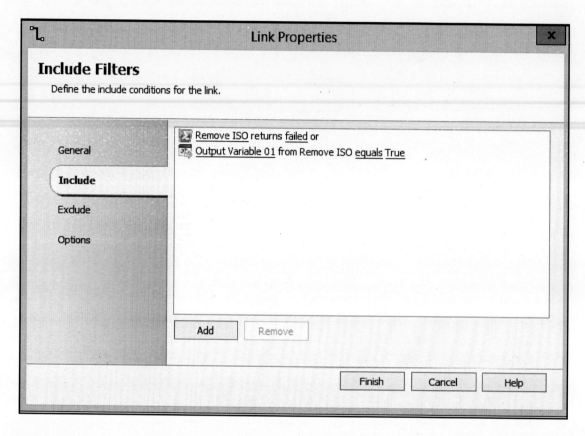

55. Click on **Finish**.
56. Click on the **Options** tab, and change the color to red.

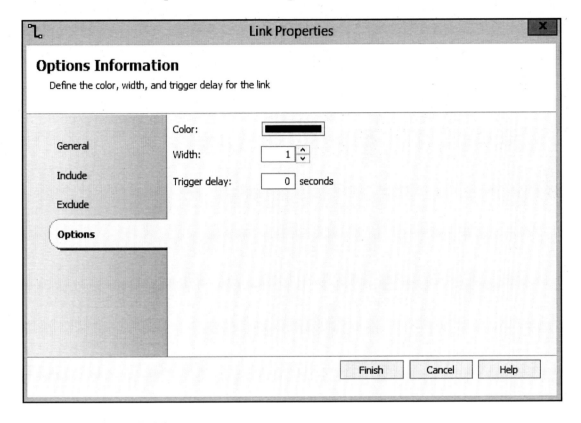

57. Click on **Finish**.

58. Double-click on the **Log Failure** activity, and provide the following information on the **Details** section:

Name of parameter	Value
Type	Error
Summary	Type the following text: `Failed to Remove ISO`
Details	• Type the following text: **Failed to Remove ISO from**. • Then, right-click on the space after the word from and navigate to **Subscribe | Published Data**. • Select **Get VM** in the **Activity** field and select **VM Name**.

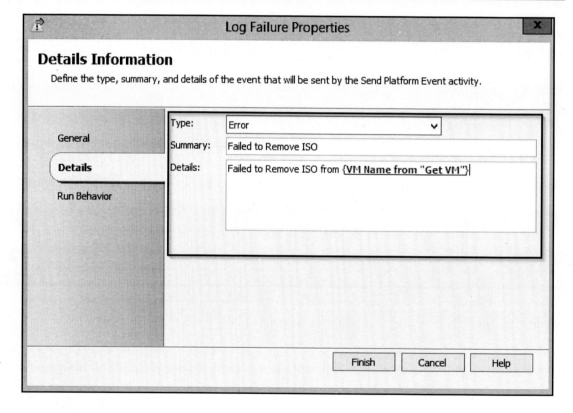

59. Click on **Finish**.

The final Runbook should look like the following screenshot:

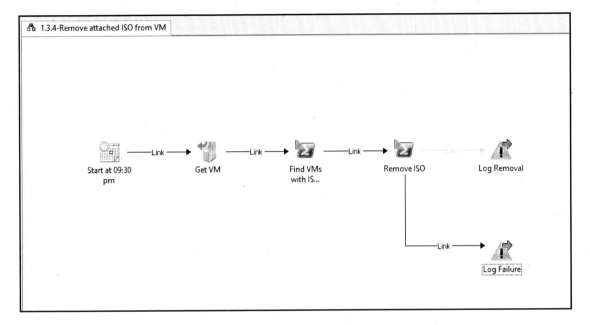

How it works...

This Runbook will run at 09:30 P.M. everyday. The Runbook retrieves and queries all the virtual machines managed by SCVMM to find any with ISO images mounted.

The Runbook will then attempt to remove any mounted ISO images. The success or failure to remove the ISO is logged.

There's more...

You have the option to change this Runbook to your specific environment, for example, the start time. You can either adjust the start time or replace it with an **Initialize Data** activity, and alternatively invoke this Runbook from another part of an automated process.

Logging events to Orchestrator

This recipe uses the **Send Platform Event** activity to log either the success or failure of the action to remove an ISO Image from a VM.

These events can be viewed in the Runbook Designer by navigating to the Runbook and selecting the **Events** tab.

However, you need access to the Runbook Designer. The Runbook can be modified to send email notifications to users without access to the Runbook Designer. An additional extension is to automatically log an incident within your service desk system.

System Center 2016 Virtual Machine Manager Integration Pack

The full set of System Center 2016 Virtual Machine Manager activities can be found at: `https://docs.microsoft.com/en-us/system-center/orchestrator/integration-pack-for-virtual-machine-manager`.

See also

Detailed information for the activities used in this Runbook can be found at the following locations:

- Microsoft TechNet—Get VM activity: `https://docs.microsoft.com/en-us/system-center/orchestrator/get-vm`
- Microsoft TechNet—Run VMM PowerShell Script activity: `https://docs.microsoft.com/en-us/system-center/orchestrator/run-vmm-powershell-script`

ConfigMgr – Automating the update Installation process

This recipe will show you how to build a Runbook to reboot your servers in during your maintenance window if an installed updates needs a reboot.

Also, it will set the server in maintenance mode will not generate an false alert in SCOM.

Getting ready

Make sure your SCCM is configured to install all the detected updates automatically on your servers.

Also make sure you have all your servers you want to finish the updates process in one collection.

You will need at least one incident for testing:

1. In the Runbook Designer, expand the connection to the SCO 2016 server.
2. Navigate to `Root\0.1-Cookbook\1.3-Chapter 5`, and create a new folder called `1.3.6-Finish Server Update Process`.

How to do it...

The following steps will show you how to configure the activities to create the Runbook for this recipe:

1. Right-click on new folder, and then click on **New** and select **Runbook**.
2. Right-click the newly created Runbook, and rename it to `1.3.6-Finish Server Update Process`.
3. Navigate to the **Activities** section in the Runbook Designer, select **Scheduling,** and drag a **Monitor Date/Time** activity into the middle pane of the Runbook (the workspace).

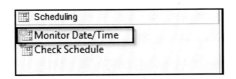

4. Right-click on the activity and choose **Rename**. Rename the activity to `Start at 02:00 AM`.
5. Right-click on the activity and choose **Properties**.
6. Change the **Interval** to `At: 02:00 AM`, and click on **Finish**.
7. Navigate to the **Activities** section in the Runbook Designer, select **SC 2016 Configuration Manager**, and drag a **Get Collection Members** activity into the middle pane of the Runbook (the workspace).

8. Double-click on the **Get Collection Members** activity and configure the **Activity** like in the Screenshot:

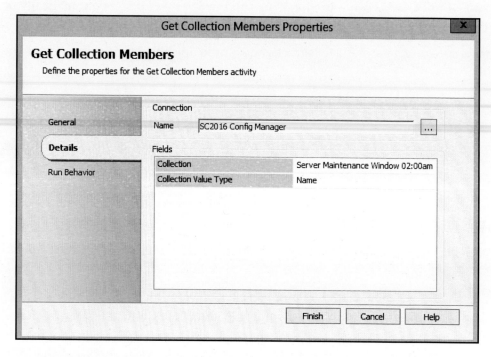

9. Click on **Finish**.

10. Navigate to the **Activities** section in the Runbook Designer, select **System**, and drag the **Query WMI** activity into the middle pane of the Runbook (the workspace):

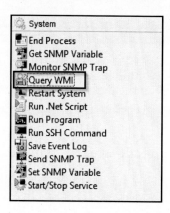

11. Rename the **Query WMI** activity to `Check Update State`.

12. Link the **Get Collection Members** activity to the **Check Update State** activity.

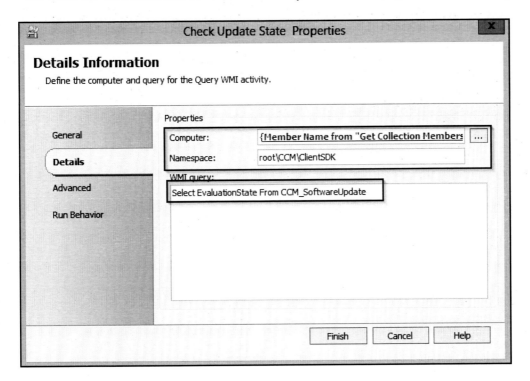

13. Click on **Finish**.

14. Right-Click on **Check Update State** activity and choose **Looping...**:

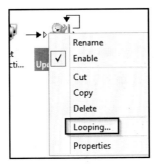

15. On the **General** tab click **Enable** and enter the Value 5 in delay between attempts.

16. At the **Exit** tab, add the following Rules:

```
WMI Query Result as a string from Check Update State does not contain
EvaluationState=0
WMI Query Result as a string from Check Update State does not contain
EvaluationState=1
WMI Query Result as a string from Check Update State does not contain
EvaluationState=2
WMI Query Result as a string from Check Update State does not contain
EvaluationState=3
WMI Query Result as a string from Check Update State does not contain
EvaluationState=4
WMI Query Result as a string from Check Update State does not contain
EvaluationState=5
WMI Query Result as a string from Check Update State does not contain
EvaluationState=6
WMI Query Result as a string from Check Update State does not contain
EvaluationState=7
WMI Query Result as a string from Check Update State contains
EvaluationState=8
WMI Query Result as a string from Check Update State contains
EvaluationState=9
WMI Query Result as a string from Check Update State matches pattern
^$
```

17. At the **Do Not Exit** tab, add the following rules:

```
WMI Query Result as a string from Check Update State contains
EvaluationState=0
WMI Query Result as a string from Check Update State contains
EvaluationState=1
WMI Query Result as a string from Check Update State contains
EvaluationState=2
WMI Query Result as a string from Check Update State contains
EvaluationState=3
WMI Query Result as a string from Check Update State contains
EvaluationState=4
WMI Query Result as a string from Check Update State contains
EvaluationState=5
WMI Query Result as a string from Check Update State contains
EvaluationState=6
WMI Query Result as a string from Check Update State contains
EvaluationState=7
```

18. Click on **Finish**.

19. Navigate to the **Activities** section in the Runbook Designer, select **Runbook Control**, and drag a **Invoke Runbook** activity into the middle pane of the Runbook (the workspace):

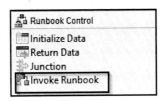

20. Rename the **Invoke Runbook** activity to `Start Maintenance Mode`.
21. Link the **Check Update State** activity to the **Start Maintenance Mode** activity.
22. Double-click on the link between **Check Update State**, the **Start Maintenance Mode** activity, and add the following include filters:

    ```
    WMI Query Result as a string from Check Update State contains
    EvaluationState=8
    WMI Query Result as a string from Check Update State contains
    EvaluationState=9
    ```

23. Next, configure the **Exclude** rules like in the Screenshot:

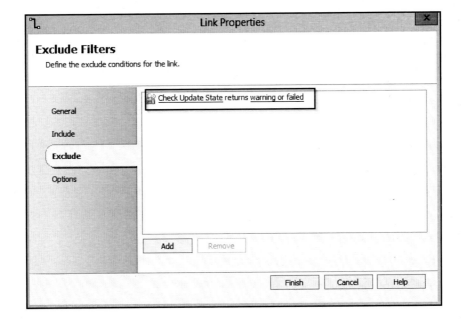

24. Click on **Finish**.

25. Double-click on the **Start Maintenance Mode** activity and select the Runbook with name **1.3.2-Activate SCOM Maintenance Mode**.

26. Configure **Activity** as shown in the screenshot:

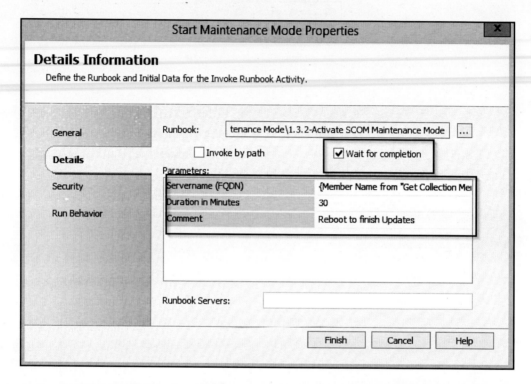

27. Click on **Finish**.

28. Navigate to the **Activities** section in the Runbook Designer, select **Runbook Control**, and drag a **Invoke Runbook** activity into the middle pane of the Runbook (the workspace):

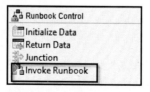

29. Rename the **Invoke Runbook** activity to `Reboot Server`.

30. Link the **Start Maintenance Mod**e activity to the **Reboot Server** activity.

31. Double-click on the **Start Maintenance Mode** activity, and select the Runbook with name **1.2.2-Reboot a Server**.

32. Configure the **Activity** as shown in the screenshot:

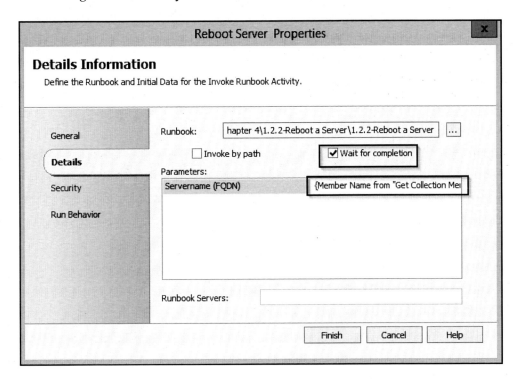

33. Click **Finish**.

34. Navigate to the **Activities** section in the Runbook Designer, select **Runbook Control**, and drag a **Invoke Runbook** activity into the middle pane of the Runbook (the workspace):

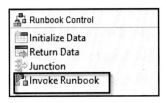

35. Rename the **Invoke Runbook** activity to **Stop Maintenance Mode**.

36. Link the **Reboot Server** activity to the **Stop Maintenance Mode** activity.

37. Double-click on the **Stop Maintenance Mode** activity and select the Runbook with name **1.3.3-Stop SCOM Maintenance Mode.**

38. Configure the activity as shown in the screenshot:

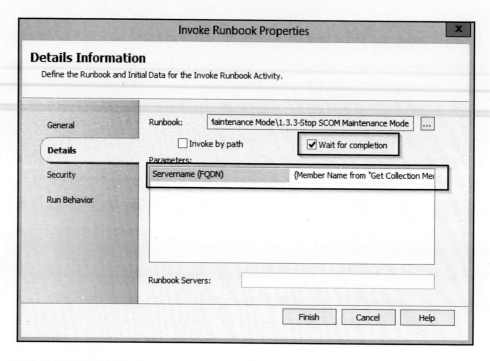

39. Click on **Finish**.

The Runbook should look like this:

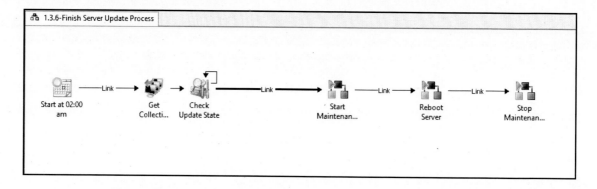

How it works...

The Runbook needs to be to run at 02:00 P.M every day.

The Runbook will read all the Members of your SCCM collection, and check the WMI query whether there are updates with a pending reboot. It is very important for that, there is a SCCM agent installed otherwise the WMI class will not be available.

Then, we call our already created Runbooks to start the maintenance mode in SCOM, reboot the server, and at the end, stop the maintenance mode.

See also

- Microsoft MSDN—WMI Evaluation State: `https://msdn.microsoft.com/en-us/library/jj155450.aspx`

- Microsoft TechNet—Get Collection Member: `https://docs.microsoft.com/en-us/system-center/orchestrator/get-collection-member`

SCSM – Raising priority, if an affected user is a VIP

Now, we will create a System Center Service Manager related Runbook to increase the priority if the affected user is a VIP. Our VIPs are all members of a special Active Directory Group.

A Runbook will monitor the creation or updating of an SCSM Incident, get the affected user, check if the user is a member of our Active Directory Group, and increase the priority by changing the impact and urgency related to our SCSM Priority Matrix.

Getting ready

This recipe will leverage System Center 2016 Service Manager to monitor your incidents.

To successfully finish this recipe, follow the recipes in `Chapter 2`, *The Initial Configuration of SCO 2016*, to register, deploy, and configure the SCSM Integration Pack.

You will need at least one incident for testing:

1. In the Runbook Designer, expand the connection to the SCO 2016 server.
2. Navigate to `Root\0.1-Cookbook\1.3-Chapter 5`, and create a new folder called `1.3.5-Raise Incident priority for VIP`.

How to do it...

After you have finished this recipe, your Service Manager Incidents will recognize your VIP Users and increase the Priority accordingly:

1. Right-click on the new folder, and then click on **New** and select **Runbook**.
2. Right-click on the newly created Runbook, and rename it to `1.3.5-Raise Incident priority for VIP`.
3. Navigate to the **Activities** section in the Runbook Designer, select **SC 2016 Service Manager**, and drag a **Monitor Object** activity into the middle pane of the Runbook (the workspace):

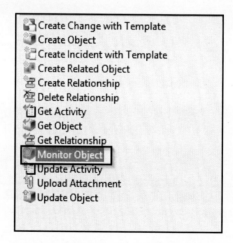

4. Double-click on the **Monitor Object**, and configure the activity like you see it in the screenshot:

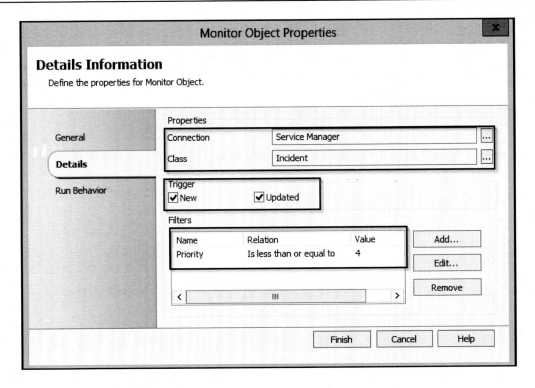

5. Click on **Finish**.
6. Navigate to the **Activities** section in the Runbook Designer, select **SC 2016 Service Manager**, and drag a **Get Relationship** activity into the middle pane of the Runbook (the workspace):

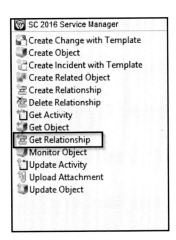

7. Rename the **Get Relationship** activity to the `Get related Users`.
8. Link the **Monitor Object** activity to the **Get related Users** activity.
9. Double-click on the **Get related Users**, and configure the activity as you see it in the screenshot:

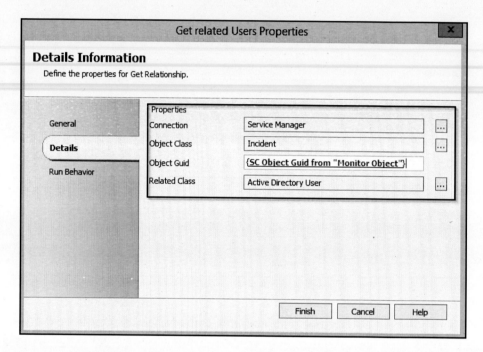

10. Click on **Finish**.
11. Navigate to the **Activities** section in the Runbook Designer, select **SC 2016 Service Manager**, and drag a **Get Object** activity into the middle pane of the Runbook (the workspace):

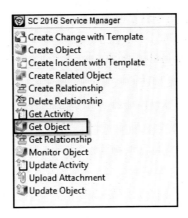

12. Rename the **Get Object** activity to **Get Affected User**.

13. Link the **Get related Users** activity to the **Get Affected User** activity.

14. Double-Click on the link between **Get related Users** activity and **Get Affected User** activity.

15. Configure the link **Include** rule like you see in the screenshot:

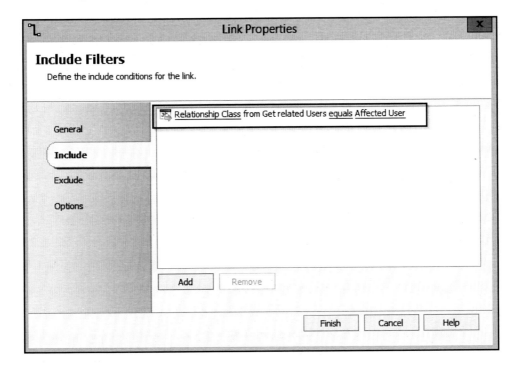

16. Click on **Finish**.
17. Next, click the **Options** tab and change the **Color** to orange.
18. Rename the link to `Relationship Class = Affected User`.
19. Click on **Finish**.
20. Double-click on the **Get Affected User** activity, and configure the activity like you see in the screenshot:

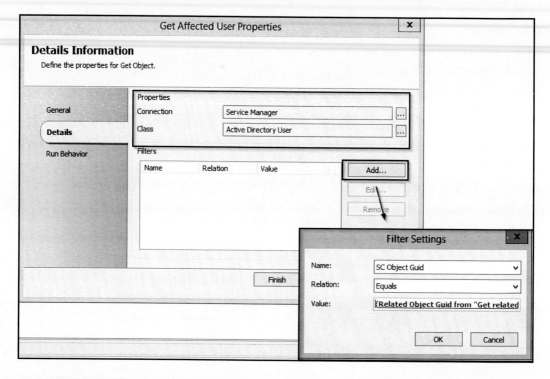

21. Click on **Finish**.
22. Navigate to the **Activities** section in the Runbook Designer, select **Active Directory**, and drag a **Get User** activity into the middle pane of the Runbook (the workspace):

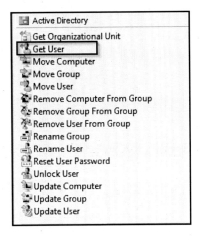

23. Link the **Get Affected User** activity to the **Get User** activity.

24. Double-click on the **Get User** activity, and configure the activity to work with your Active Directory by selecting a configuration.

25. Switch to the **Filters** tab and configure the filter like this:

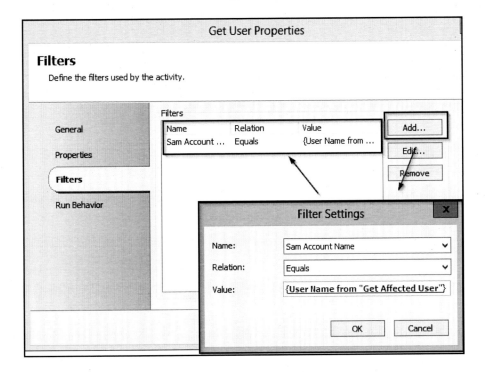

26. Click on **Finish**.

27. Navigate to the **Activities** section in the Runbook Designer, select Active Directory and drag a **Get Group** activity into the middle pane of the Runbook (the workspace):

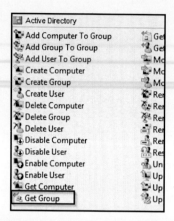

28. Rename the **Get Group** activity to Get VIP Group activity.

29. Link the **Get User** activity to the **Get VIP Group** activity.

30. Double-click on the **Get VIP Group** activity and configure the activity to work with your Active Directory by selecting a configuration.

31. Switch to the **Filters** tab and configure the filter like this:

Name	Relation	Value
Member	Equals	{Distinguished Name from "get User"}
Sam Account Name	Equals	Your Group Sam Account Name, in our Example, Company-VIP

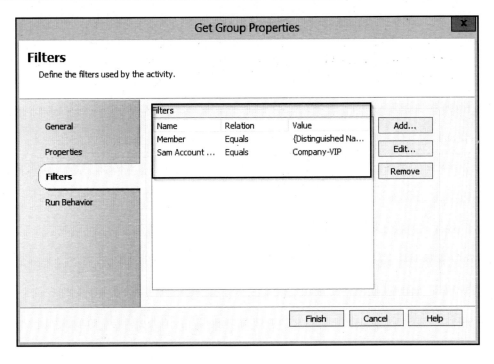

32. Click on **Finish**.
33. Navigate to the **Activities** section in the Runbook Designer, select **SC 2016 Service Manager**, and drag a **Update Object** activity into the middle pane of the Runbook (the workspace):

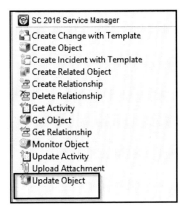

34. Rename the **Update Object** activity to `Set INC Priority to 3` activity.
35. Link the **Get Group** activity to the **Set INC Priority to 3** activity.
36. Double-click on the link between **Get Group** activity to the **Set INC Priority to 3** activity, and configure the **Include** filter like in this screenshot:

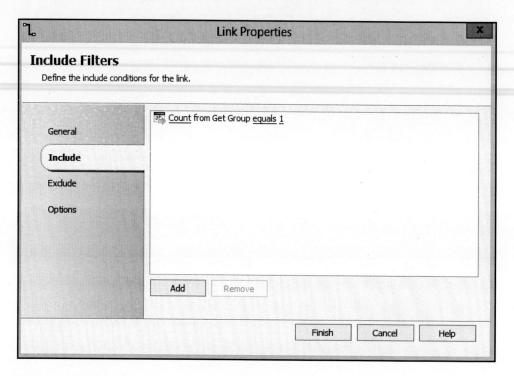

37. Click on **Finish**.
38. Rename the link to `Group Count = 1`.
39. Set the color of the link to orange.

40. Double-click on the **Set INC Priority to 3** activity and configure the activity like in this screenshot:

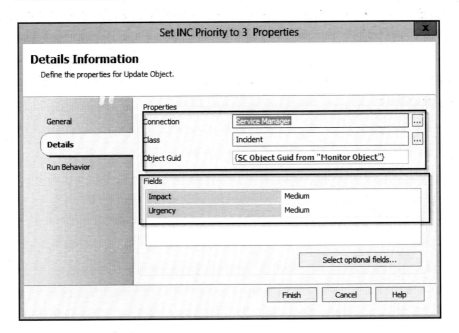

The Runbook should look like this:

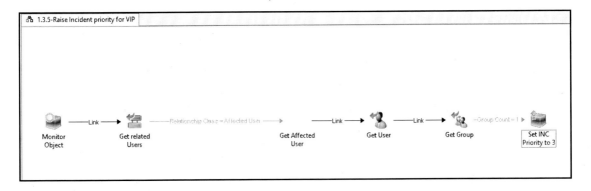

How it works...

The Runbook needs to be checked in and in Run State to monitor every incident update.

The **Get Related Users** activity will return all the related users for this incident, also the created by and the assigned to, so it is very important to limit the link filter after the activity to only forward the affected User.

As we have configured the `1.2.1.1-Add Users to Group` Runbook in `Chapter 4,` *Building Advanced Runbooks*, we also configured the link filer between **Get Group** activity to the **Set INC Priority to 3** activity to only call the next activity if the user is in our VIP group.

The **Set INC Priority to 3** activity needs to be adjusted to meet your SCSM **Priority Calculation**; for example, see the screenshot in our environment to understand why we have chosen the selected **Impact** and **Urgency**:

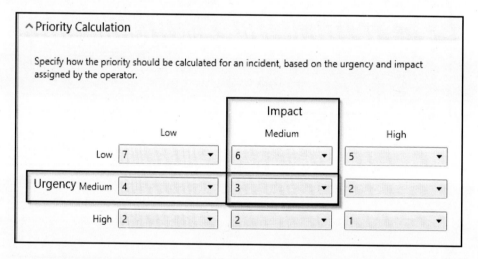

See also

Detailed information for the activities used in this Runbook can be found at the following locations:

- Microsoft TechNet—Get Object: `https://docs.microsoft.com/en-us/system-center/orchestrator/get-object`
- Microsoft TechNet—Update Object: `https://docs.microsoft.com/en-us/system-center/orchestrator/update-object`
- Microsoft TechNet—Get Relationship: `https://docs.microsoft.com/en-us/system-center/orchestrator/get-relationship`

6
Advanced Runbooks for Your Daily Tasks

In this chapter, we will be providing recipes on how to build advanced Runbooks to automate your daily tasks

- Active Directory – Sending an email to users if their password will expire soon
- SCOM – Advanced alerting with SCO

Introduction

Now it's time to make some cool stuff, after creating our first simple Runbooks, let's now build some advanced Runbooks which will help you in your daily business.

Active Directory – Sending an email to users if their password will expire soon

You can schedule a Runbook in System Center 2016 Orchestrator to automatically notify your users before their passwords expire.

The business process of this workflow is defined in the following diagram:

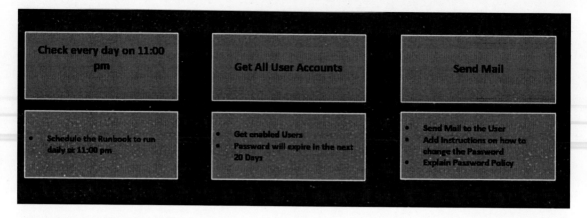

Getting ready

To get ready for our next Runbook we need to create a new folder and, a new Runbook in the Runbook Designer:

1. In the Runbook Designer expand the connection to the SCO 2016 server.
2. Navigate to `Root\0.1-Cookbook` and create a new folder called `1.4-Chapter 6`.
3. Create a subfolder called `1.4.1-Send Password expire Mail`.
4. Right-click on the new folder and then click on **New** and select **Runbook**.
5. Right-click the newly created Runbook and rename it to **1.4.1-Send Password expire Mail**.

How to do it...

This Runbook requires a schedule, which is the first activity we need in our Runbook:

1. In the newly created Runbook navigate to and click on **Scheduling** under **Activities** and then select and drag a **Monitor Date/Time** activity into the middle pane of the Runbook:

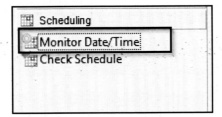

2. Double-click on the **Monitor Date/Time** activity. Configure the interval in the Details section using the information in the following table:

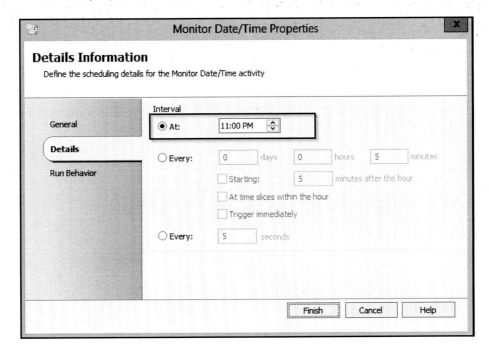

3. Click on **Finish**.

4. Navigate to the **Activities** section and click on **System,** select and drag a **Run .Net Script** activity into the middle pane of the Runbook next to the **Monitor Date/Time** activity:

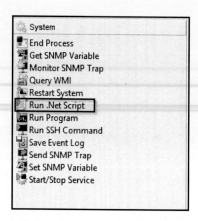

5. Link the **Monitor Date/Time** activity to the **Run .Net Script** activity.
6. Rename the **Run .Net Script** activity to **Get Users and Days till expire**.
7. Double-click on the **Get Users and Days till expire** activity and select PowerShell in the **Language | Type** field on the **Details** section (use the **...** button to select).
8. Right-click in the **Script** field and select **Expand** to open up the **Script** field. Add the following code into the **Script** field:

```
#Import Active Directory Module
Import-Module ActiveDirectory
#Day of Span, to limit the Result
$SpanDays="20"
#Settings
$Displayname=@()
$Mail=@()
$Days=@()
$Sam=@()
$DN=@()
#Get all Users which are enabled and Password will expire
$Users=Get-ADUser -filter {(Enabled -eq $True) -and
(PasswordNeverExpires -eq $False)} -Properties DisplayName,
msDS-UserPasswordExpiryTimeComputed, Mail, samaccountname,
distinguishedName | Where-Object {$_.DisplayName -ne $null} |
Select Mail, samaccountname,distinguishedName,
DisplayName,@{Name="ExpiryDate";Expression=
{([datetime]::fromfiletime($_."msDS-
UserPasswordExpiryTimeComputed")).DateTime}}
```

```
#Go through each User and check if password will expire in the
next XX Days, see Span configuration
foreach ($Entry in $Users) {
     $Span=NEW-TIMESPAN -Start (Get-Date) -End
(Get-date($Entry.ExpiryDate))
   if ($Span -le $SpanDays -and $Span -gt 0) {
       $Displayname+=$entry.DisplayName
       $Mail+=$Entry.Mail
         $Days+=$span.Days
       $SAM+=$Entry.samaccountname
       $DN+=$Entry.distinguishedName
   }
}
```

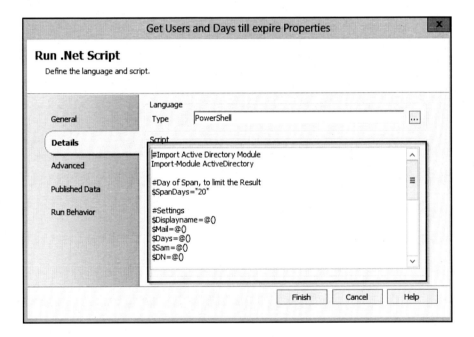

9. Click **OK**.

10. Next, navigate to the **Published Data** tab and configure like you see in the screenshot below:

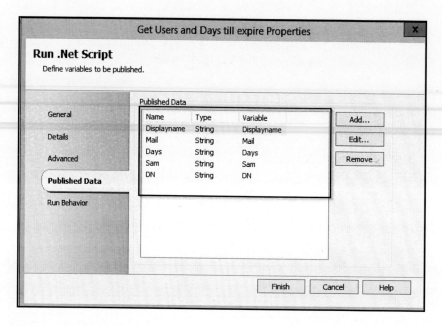

11. Click **Finish**.

12. Navigate to the **Activities** section and click on **Email,** select and drag a **Send Email** activity into the middle pane of the Runbook next to the **Get Users and Days till expire** activity:

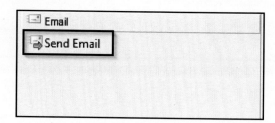

13. Link the **Get Users and Days till expire** activity to the **Send Mail** activity.

14. Double-click the **Send Mail** activity.
15. Enter this in the **Subject:** Instructions for changing the password.
16. Add a recipient like you see in the screenshot:

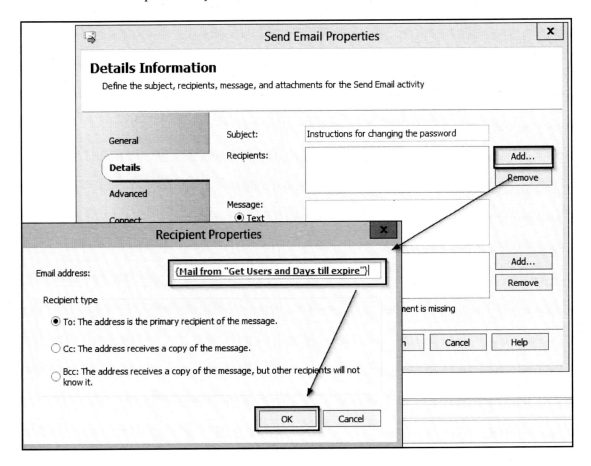

17. Right-click on the **Message** field and select **Expand** to open up the **Message** field. Type in the following:

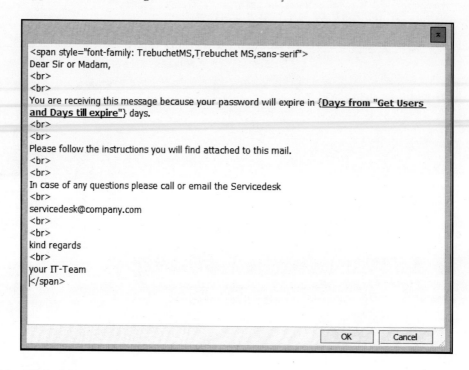

18. Click **OK**.

19. In the **Attachment Properties**, select the instructions file that you have created:

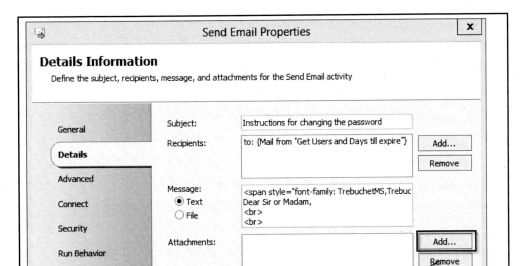

20. Switch to the **Advanced and Connect** tab to configure the activity to fit your SMTP environment. Make sure the activity can send an email successfully.
21. Click **Finish**.
22. Double-click the link present between the **Get Users and Days till expire** activity and, the **Send Mail** activity.

23. Configure the **Include Filter** like you see it in the following screenshot:

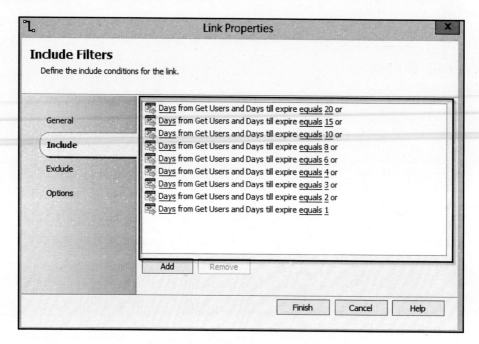

24. Rename the filter to send emails on specific days.
25. Change the link color to orange by navigating to the **Options** tab.
26. Click **Finish**.
27. Navigate to the **Activities** section and click on **Scheduling,** select and drag a **Check Schedule** activity into the middle pane of the Runbook beyond the **Get Users and Days till expire** activity:

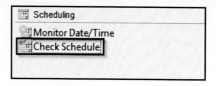

28. Link the **Get Users and Days till expire** activity to the **Check Schedule** activity.
29. Rename the **Check Schedule** activity to On Monday.

30. On the left pane, navigate to **Global Settings** and **Schedule**.
31. Right-click in the middle pane and select **New...** and **Schedule**:

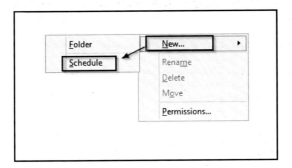

32. Enter the name Only on Monday to the **Name** property.
33. Under the **Details** tab change the configuration according to the screenshot:

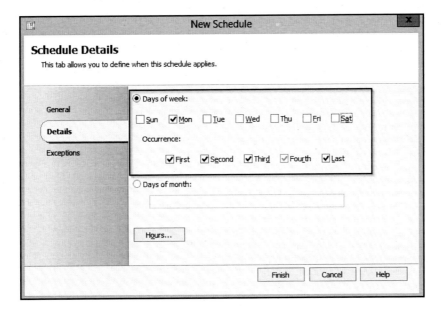

34. Click **Finish**.
35. Navigate back to the Runbook 1.4.1–Send Password expire Mail and double click the **On Monday** activity.

36. In the **Schedule Template** select the newly created schedule **Only on Monday**:

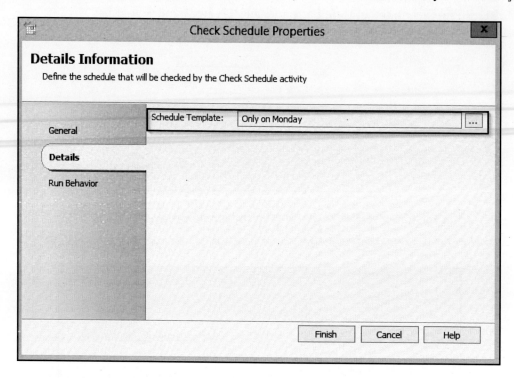

37. Click **Finish**.
38. Navigate to the **Activities** section and click on **Text File Management,** select and drag the **Append Line** activity into the middle pane of the Runbook next to the **On Monday** activity:

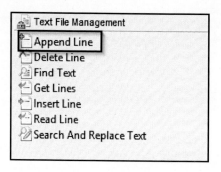

39. Link the **Get Users and Days till expire** activity to the **Append Line** activity.
40. Rename the **Append Line** activity to **Write File for Servicedesk**.
41. Double-click the **Write File for Servicedesk** activity.
42. Select a path where the file should be stored and select **Auto** as file encoding value.
43. Right-click on the text field and select expand to open up the text field. Type in the following:

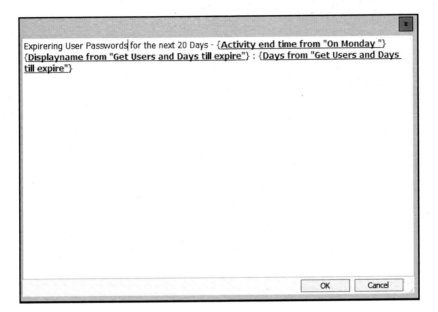

44. Click **OK**.
45. Click **Finish**.
46. Double-click the link present between **On Monday** activity and **Write File for Servicedesk** activity.

47. Configure the **Include** rule like you see it in the screenshot:

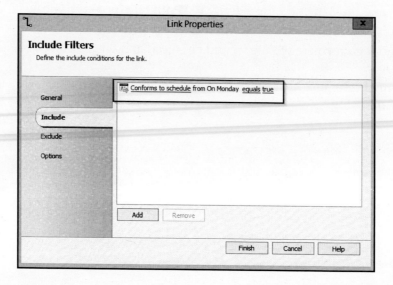

48. Change the color of the link to orange.
49. Click **Finish**.

The Runbook should look like this:

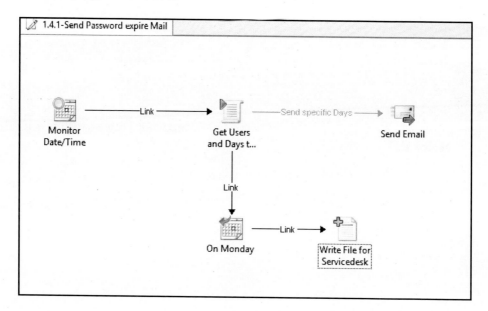

How it works...

This Runbook needs to be checked in and started (Run) so as to execute it. Though the Runbook is running, the actions will only be executed at the specified time in the schedule. In this example it will start at 11:00 P.M. every day (**Monitor Date/Time** activity).

The PowerShell activity will query all the active users whose passwords will expire within the next 20 Days.

We will also be saving a TXT file on each Monday to assist our helpdesk. The helpdesk will be able to read this list and be prepared for a User that may call to inquire about their password expiring.

See also

Detailed information on the activities used in this Runbook can be found here:

- Microsoft Technet – Monitor Date/Time activity: `http://technet.microsoft.com/en-us/library/hh225031.aspx`
- Microsoft Technet – Run .Net Script activity: `http://technet.microsoft.com/en-us/library/hh206103.aspx`
- Microsoft Technet – Append Line activity: `http://technet.microsoft.com/en-us/library/hh206072.aspx`

SCOM – Advanced alerting with SCO

In this recipe, we will create multiple Runbooks. This has to be done because, tasks can be very complicated and powerful, so we will split as much task as possible among separate Runbooks.

We will create a full function SCOM alerting, to send notifications to business service owners, technical accounts, and external helpline.

The business process of this workflow is defined in the following diagram:

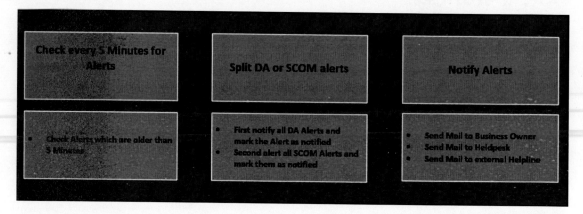

Refer to the diagram about Runbooks as well:

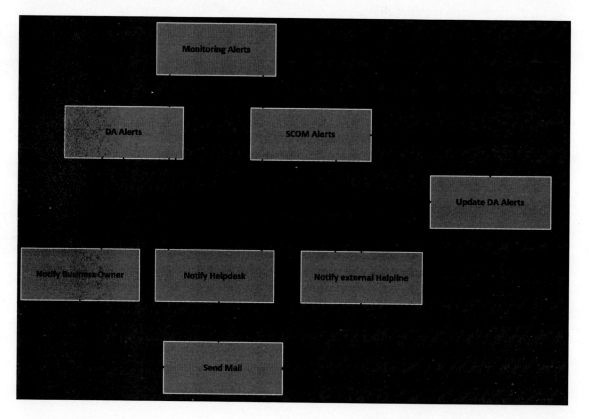

Getting ready

To successfully complete this recipe you will need a System Center Operations Manager 2016 environment with at least one configured distributed application.

For our example we will be using a distributed application called **DA_Mailservice**. For this, we will create one Active Directory Group to get our business service owner and our service desk members related to that business service.

So we first create an Active Directory Group called `BS_MailService`. Then configure the business service owner as the Manager, and add the service desk members to the group:

1. In the Runbook Designer, expand the connection to the SCO 2016 server.
2. Navigate to `Root\0.1-Cookbook\1.4-Chapter 6` and create a new folder called `1.4.2-SCOM Alerting`.
3. Create the following subfolders:
     - `1.4.2.1-DA-Alert`
     - `1.4.2.2-SCOM-Alert`
     - `1.4.2.3-Notify Business Owner`
     - `1.4.2.4-Notify Helpdesk`
     - `1.4.2.5-Notify external Helpline`
     - `1.4.2.6-Send Mail`
     - `1.4.2.7-Update DA Alerts`

4. Make sure your folders look like this:

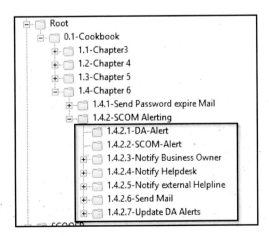

Also, make sure you have created the following resolution states in SCOM:

Name	ID
SCO	100
Notified	101

Lastly, we need to create a SQL View on your SCOM Database called `z_Alert_DA_View` with the following SQL Query:

```
SELECT           dbo.AlertView.Id AS AlertID, dbo.AlertView.ResolutionState,
Rel3.DisplayName AS DA
FROM             dbo.AlertView INNER JOIN
                        dbo.Relationship AS Rel1 ON
dbo.AlertView.MonitoringObjectId = Rel1.TargetEntityId INNER JOIN
                        dbo.Relationship AS Rel2 ON Rel1.SourceEntityId =
Rel2.TargetEntityId INNER JOIN
                        dbo.BaseManagedEntity AS Rel3 ON
Rel2.SourceEntityId = Rel3.BaseManagedEntityId
WHERE         (dbo.AlertView.LanguageCode = 'ENU') AND (Rel3.FullName LIKE
'Service_%')
```

How to do it...

We will start with the Runbooks from bottom to the top, so follow this recipe till the end to get a complete SCOM Alerting Runbooks Solution.

Update DA Alerts Runbook

1. Navigate to the folder `1.4.2.7-Update DA Alerts`.
2. Right-click on the folder and then click on **New** and select **Runbook**.
3. Right-click the newly created Runbook and rename it to **1.4.7-Update DA Alerts**.
4. Navigate to the **Activities** section in the Runbook Designer. Click on **Runbook Control**, and select and drag the **Initialize Data** activity to the middle pane of the Runbook (start from the leftmost part of the pane and work your way to the right as you add additional activities):

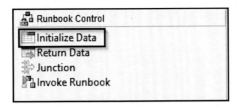

5. Right-click on **Initialize Data** | **Properties**. Click on **Add** and use the following table to configure the parameters in the **Details** section by clicking on each of them. Click on **Finish**:

Name of parameter	Data type	Contains information
NewResolutionState	String	Contains the new resolution state for our SCOM Alerts
OrigResolutionState	String	Contains the original resolution state for our SCOM Alerts
DA_Name	String	Contains the distributed application name

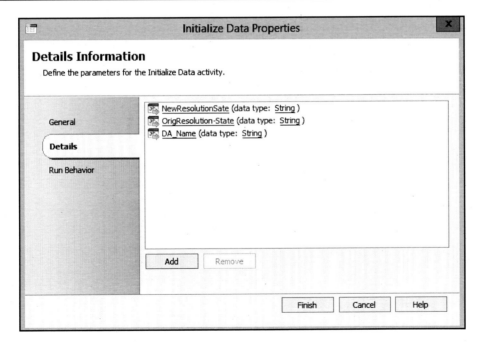

6. Click on **Finish**.

7. Navigate to the **Activities** section, click on **System**, and drag the **Run .Net Script** activity into the middle pane of the Runbook next to the **Initialize Data** activity:

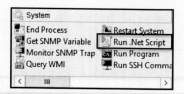

8. Link the **Initialize Data** activity to the **Run .Net Script** activity.

9. Rename the **Run .Net Script** activity to `Update DA Alerts`.

10. Double-click on the **Update DA Alerts** activity and select **PowerShell** in the **Language | Type** field on the **Details** section (use the **...** button to select).

11. Right-click in the **Script** field and select **Expand** to open up the **Script** field. Add the code shown in the following screenshot into the **Script** field:

12. Click **OK** and click **Finish**.

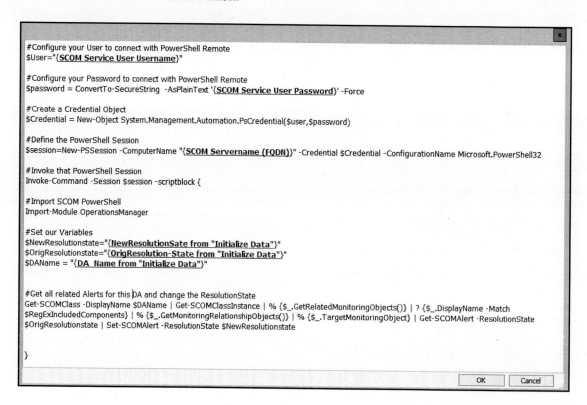

```
#Configure your User to connect with PowerShell Remote
$User="{SCOM Service User Username}"

#Configure your Password to connect with PowerShell Remote
$password = ConvertTo-SecureString  -AsPlainText '{SCOM Service User Password}' -Force

#Create a Credential Object
$Credential = New-Object System.Management.Automation.PsCredential($user,$password)

#Define the PowerShell Session
$session=New-PSSession -ComputerName "{SCOM Servername (FQDN)}" -Credential $Credential -ConfigurationName Microsoft.PowerShell32

#Invoke that PowerShell Session
Invoke-Command -Session $session -scriptblock {

#Import SCOM PowerShell
Import-Module OperationsManager

#Set our Variables
$NewResolutionstate="{NewResolutionSate from "Initialize Data"}"
$OrigResolutionstate="{OrigResolution-State from "Initialize Data"}"
$DAName = "{DA_Name from "Initialize Data"}"


#Get all related Alerts for this DA and change the ResolutionState
Get-SCOMClass -DisplayName $DAName | Get-SCOMClassInstance | % {$_.GetRelatedMonitoringObjects()} | ? {$_.DisplayName -Match
$RegExIncludedComponents} | % {$_.GetMonitoringRelationshipObjects()} | % {$_.TargetMonitoringObject} | Get-SCOMAlert -ResolutionState
$OrigResolutionstate | Set-SCOMAlert -ResolutionState $NewResolutionstate

}
```

The Runbook should look like this:

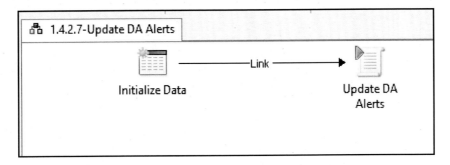

Send mail Runbook

This Runbook will send an E-Mail only, it will be built, that it also can be used for other Processes and Runbooks:

1. Navigate to the folder `1.4.2.6-Send Mail`.
2. Right-click on the folder and then click on **New** and select **Runbook**.
3. Right-click the newly created Runbook and rename it to `1.4.6-Send Mail`.
4. Navigate to the `Activities` section in the Runbook Designer. Click on **Runbook Control**, and select and drag the **Initialize Data** activity to the middle pane of the Runbook (start from the leftmost part of the pane and work your way to the right as you add additional activities).

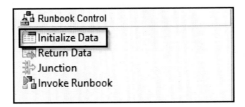

5. Right-click on **Initialize Data | Properties**. Click on **Add** and use the following table to configure the parameters in the **Details** section by clicking on each of them. Click on **Finish**.

Name of parameter	Data type	Contains information
Recipient Mail	String	Contains the recipient mail address to send the email to
Subject	String	Contains the subject of our email
Body	String	Contains the body of our email

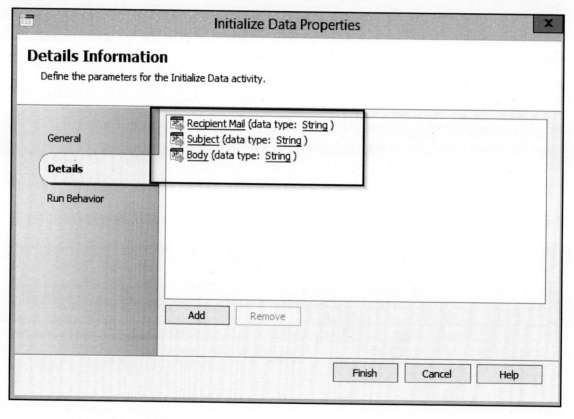

6. Click on **Finish**.
7. Navigate to the **Activities** section, click on email and drag a **Send Email** activity into the middle pane of the Runbook next to the **Initialize Data** activity:

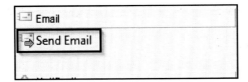

8. Link the **Initialize Data** activity to the **Send Email** activity.
9. Double-click on the **Send Email** activity and configure the **Send** tab like this screenshot:

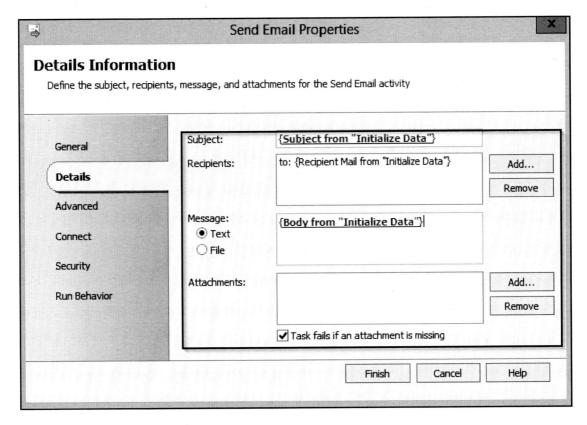

10. Navigate through the **Advanced and Connect** tab to configure this activity so that it will be able to send an email in your environment:
11. Click **Finish**.

Your Runbook should look like this:

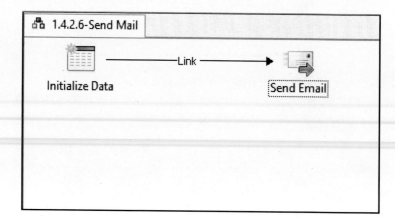

Notify external helpline Runbook

This Runbook will determine the external Helpline to send an email. This will be used only for urgent Alerts:

1. Navigate to the folder 1.4.2.5-Notify external Helpline.
2. Right-click on the Folder and then click on New and select Runbook
3. Right-click the newly created Runbook and rename it to 1.4.5-Notify external Helpline.
4. Navigate to the **Activities** section in the Runbook Designer. Click on **Runbook Control**, and select and drag an **Initialize Data** activity to the middle pane of the Runbook (start from the leftmost part of the pane and work your way to the right as you add additional activities):

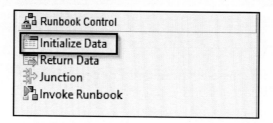

5. Right-click on **Initialize Data | Properties**. Click on **Add** and use the following table to configure the parameters in the **Details** section by clicking on each of them. Click on **Finish**.

Name of parameter	Data type	Contains information
Business Service Name	String	Contains the Business Service Name to decide to which external partner we would like to send the email
Alert Title	String	Contains the alert title of our email
Alert Description	String	Contains the alert description of our email

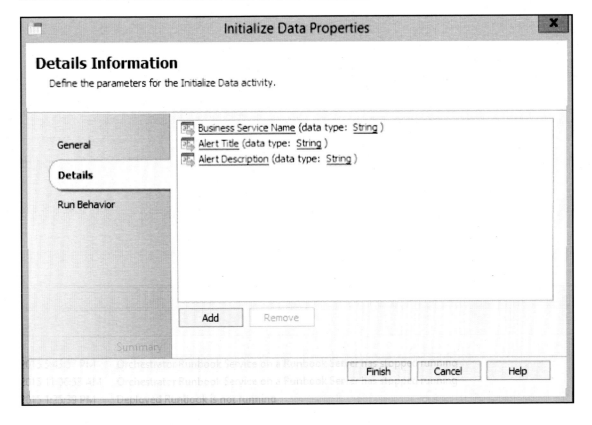

6. Click on **Finish**.

7. Navigate to the **Activities** section, click on **Utilities** and drag a **Map Published Data** activity into the middle pane of the Runbook next to the **Initialize Data** activity:

8. Link the **Initialize Data** activity to the **Map Published Data** activity.
9. Rename the **Map Published Data** activity to **Decide external Partner**.
10. Double-click on the **Decide external Partner** activity and configure like in the screenshot:

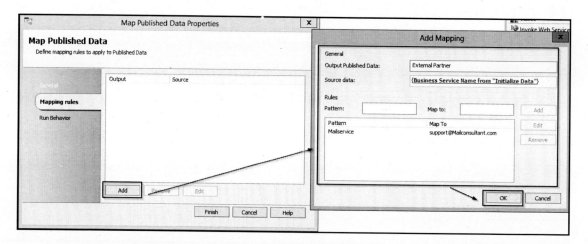

11. Click on **Finish**.
12. Navigate to the **Activities** section, click on **Runbook Control** and drag the **Invoke Runbook** activity into the middle pane of the Runbook next to the **Decide external Partner** activity:

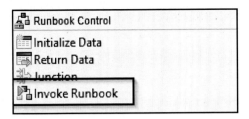

13. Link the **Decide external Partner** activity to the **Invoke Runbook** activity.
14. Double-click on the **Invoke Runbook** activity and select the **1.4.2.6-Send Mail** Runbook and configure like in the screenshot:

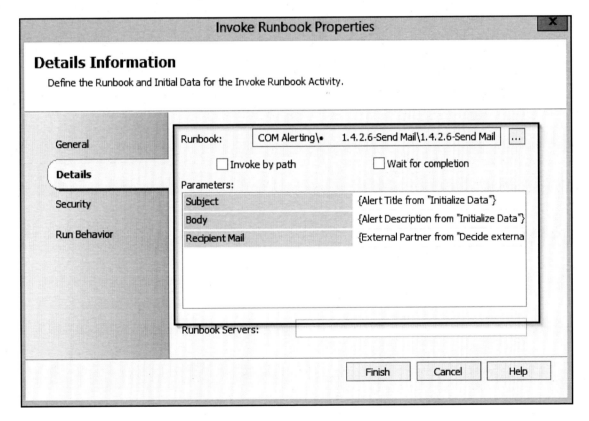

15. Click **Finish**.
16. Rename the **Invoke Runbook** activity to **Send external Mail**.
17. Double-click the link between **Decide external Partner** activity and **Send external Mail** activity.

18. Configure the **Include** rule like shown in this screenshot:

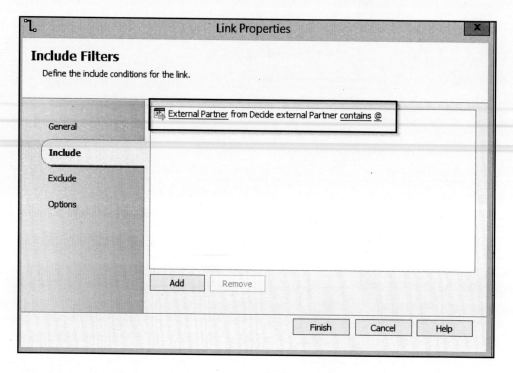

19. Rename the link to **only if Mail found** and change the color to orange
20. Click **Finish**.

The Runbook should look like this:

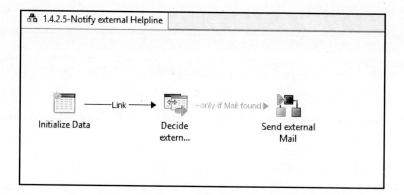

Notify Helpdesk Runbook

The Runbook will notify our helpdesk, related to the Business Service and the members of the Active Directory Group:

1. Navigate to the folder `1.4.2.4-Notify Helpdesk`.
2. Right-click on the folder and then click on **New** and select **Runbook**.
3. Right-click the newly created Runbook and rename it to **1.4.4-Notify Helpdesk**.
4. Navigate to the **Activities** section in the Runbook Designer. Click on **Runbook Control**, and select and drag the **Initialize Data** activity to the middle pane of the Runbook (start from the leftmost part of the pane and work towards the right as you add additional activities):

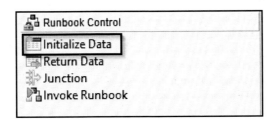

5. Right-click the **Initialize Data** and select **Properties**. Click on **Add** and use the following table to configure the parameters in the **Details** section by clicking on each of them in turn. Click on **Finish**.

Name of parameter	Data type	Contains information
Business Service Name	String	Contains the business service name to decide to which external partner we would like to send the email
Alert Title	String	Contains the alert title for our email
Alert Description	String	Contains the alert description for our email

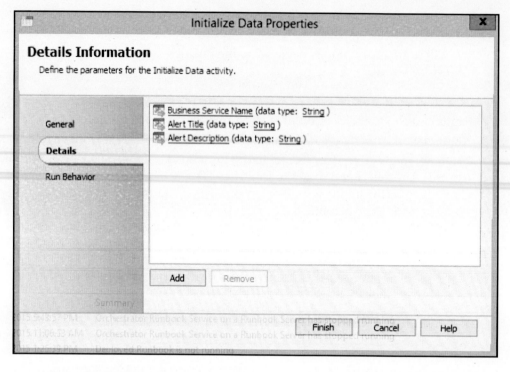

6. Click on **Finish**.
7. Navigate to the **Activities** section, click on **Active Directory** and drag a **Get Group** activity into the middle pane of the Runbook next to the **Initialize Data** activity.

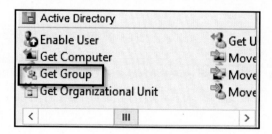

8. Link the **Initialize Data** activity to the **Get Group** activity.
9. Rename the **Get Group** activity to **Get Business Service Group**.
10. Double-click the **Get Business Service Group** activity and configure the connection to work with your **Active Directory**.
11. Switch to the **Filters** tab and configure like in the screenshot:

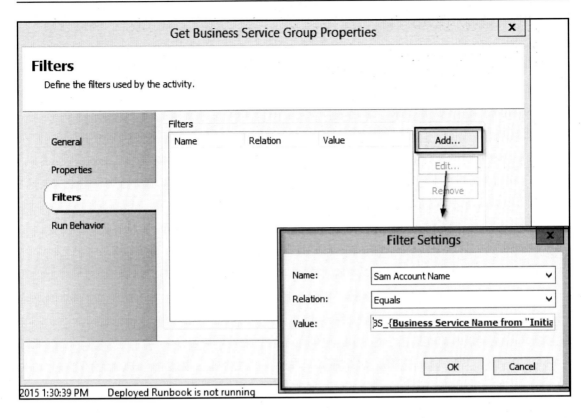

12. Click **Finish**.
13. Navigate to the **Activities** section, click on **Active Directory** and drag a **Get User** activity into the middle pane of the Runbook next to the **Get Business Service Group** activity:

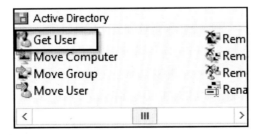

14. Link the **Get Business Service Group** activity to the **Get User** activity.
15. Rename the **Get User** activity to **Get Business Service Group Members**.
16. Double-click the **Get Business Service Group Members** activity and configure the connection to work with your Active Directory.

17. Switch to the **Filters** tab and configure like in the screenshot:

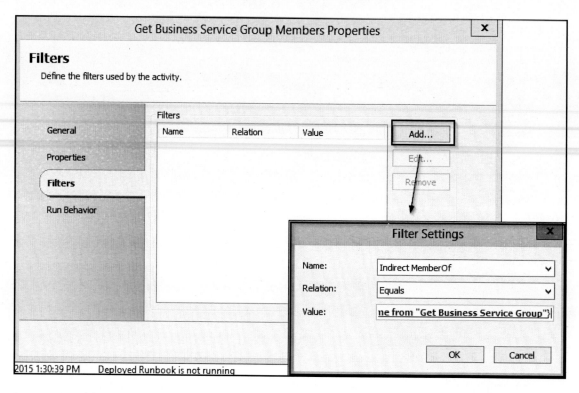

18. Click **Finish**.
19. Navigate to the **Activities** section, click on **Runbook Control** and drag the **Invoke Runbook** activity into the middle pane of the Runbook next to the **Get Business Service Group Members** activity:

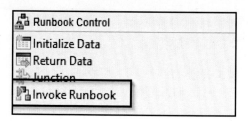

20. Link the **Get Business Service Group Members** activity to the **Invoke Runbook** activity.

21. Double-click on the **Invoke Runbook** activity and select the **1.4.2.6-Send Mail Runbook** and configure like in the screenshot:

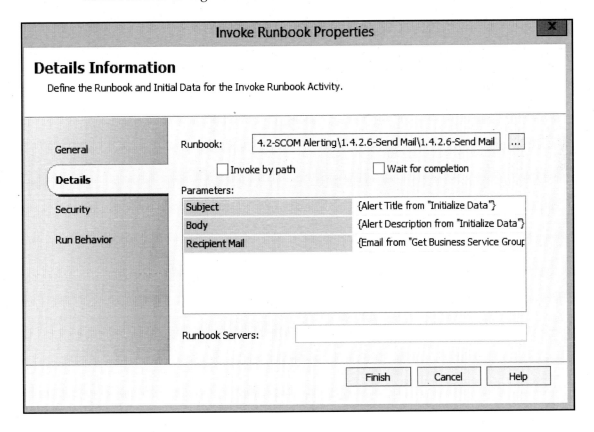

22. Click **Finish**.

23. Rename the **Invoke Runbook** activity to `Send Helpdesk Mail`.

24. Double-click the link between **Get Business Service Group Members** activity and **Send Helpdesk Mail** activity.

25. Configure the **Include** rule like in the screenshot:

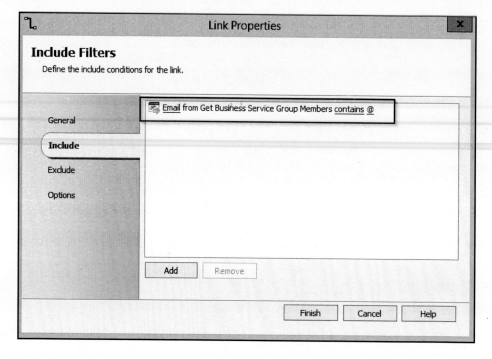

26. Rename the link to **only if Mail found** and change the color to orange.
27. Click **Finish**.

The Runbook should look like this:

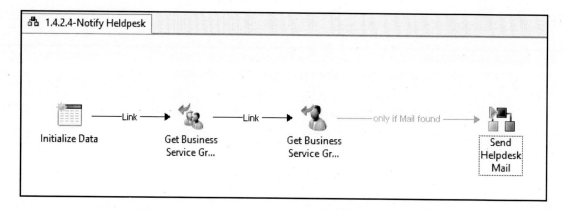

Notify Business Owner Runbook

After you have finished the steps here, the Runbook will send an email to the business owner. The Business Owner will be determined from Active Directory.

1. Navigate to the folder `1.4.2.3-Notify Business Owner`.
2. Right-click on the folder and then click on **New** and select **Runbook**.
3. Right-click the newly created Runbook and rename it to **1.4.2.3-Notify Business Owner**.
4. Navigate to the **Activities** section in the Runbook Designer. Click on **Runbook Control**, and select and drag an **Initialize Data** activity to the middle pane of the Runbook (start from the leftmost part of the pane and move to the right as you add additional activities):

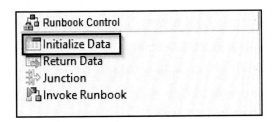

5. Right-click on **Initialize Data** | **Properties**. Click on **Add** and use the following table to configure the parameter in the **Details** section by clicking on each of the parameters in turn. Click on **Finish**.

Name of parameter	Data type	Contains information
Business Service Name	String	Contains the business service name from which we can decide the external partner we would like to send the email
Alert Title	String	Contains the alert title for our email
Alert Description	String	Contains the alert description for our email

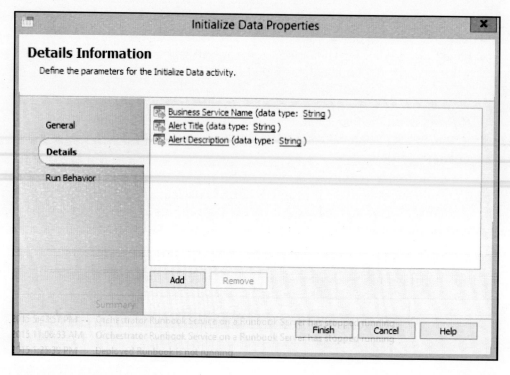

6. Click on **Finish**.
7. Navigate to the **Activities** section, click on **Active Directory** and drag the **Get Group** activity into the middle pane of the Runbook next to the **Initialize Data** activity:

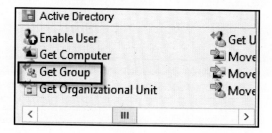

8. Link the **Initialize Data** activity to the **Get Group** activity.
9. Rename the **Get Group** activity to **Get Business Service Group**.
10. Double-click the **Get Business Service Group** activity and configure the connection to work with your Active Directory.
11. Switch to the **Filters** tab and configure like in the screenshot:

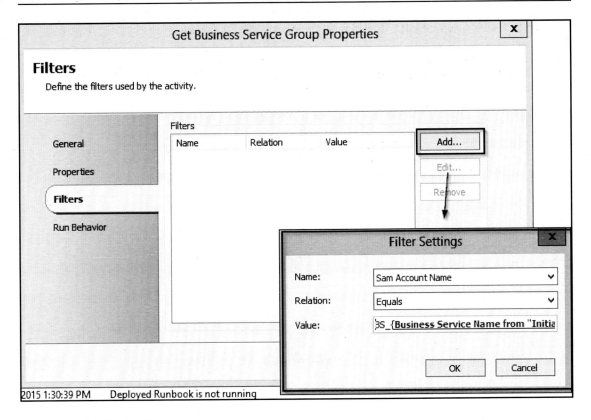

12. Click **Finish**.
13. Navigate to the **Activities** section, click on **Active Directory** and drag the **Get User** activity into the middle pane of the Runbook next to the **Get Business Service Group** activity:

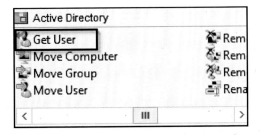

14. Link the **Get Business Service Group** activity to the **Get User** activity.
15. Rename the **Get User** activity to **Get Business Service Owner**.
16. Double-click the **Get Business Service Owner** activity and configure the connection to work with your Active Directory.

17. Configure the **Properties** like you see in the screenshot:

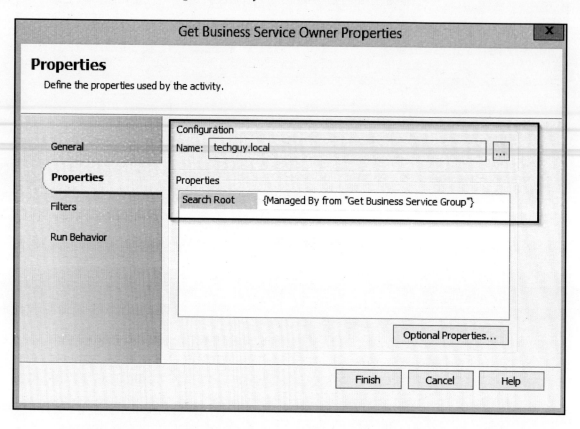

18. Click **Finish**.
19. Navigate to the **Activities** section, click on **Runbook Control** and drag the **Invoke Runbook** activity into the middle pane of the Runbook next to the **Get Business Service Owner** activity:

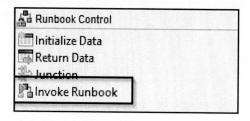

20. Link the **Get Business Service Owner** activity to the **Invoke Runbook** activity.

21. Double-click the **Invoke Runbook** activity and select the **1.4.2.6-Send Mail Runbook** and configure like in the screenshot:

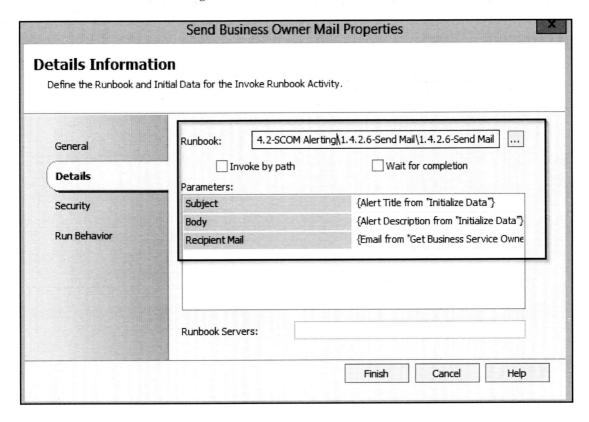

22. Click **Finish**.

23. Rename the **Invoke Runbook** activity to **Send Business Owner Mail**.

24. Double-click the link between **Get Business Service Group Members** activity and **Send Helpdesk Mail** activity.

25. Configure the **Include** rule like in this screenshot:

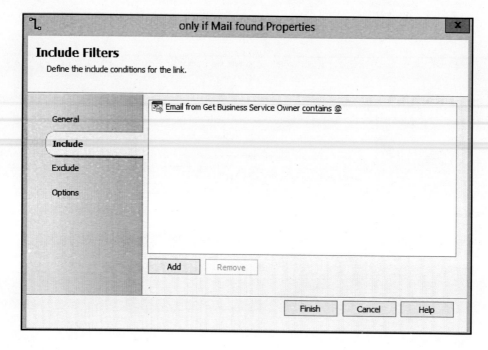

26. Rename the link to `only if Mail found` and change the color to orange.
27. Click **Finish**.

The Runbook should look like this:

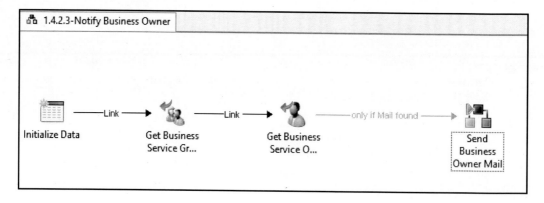

Notify SCOM-Alert

This Runbook will send a SCOM Alert Notification related to the Alert:

1. Navigate to the folder `1.4.2.2-SCOM-Alert`.
2. Right-click on the folder and then click on **New** and select **Runbook**.
3. Right-click the newly created Runbook and rename it to **1.4.2.2-SCOM-Alert**.
4. Navigate to the **Activities** section in the Runbook Designer. Click on **Runbook Control**, and select and drag the **Initialize Data** activity to the middle pane of the Runbook (start from the leftmost part of the pane and work towards the right as you add additional activities):

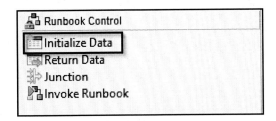

5. Right-click on **Initialize Data** | **Properties**. Click on **Add** and use the following table to configure the parameters in the **Details** section by clicking on each of the parameters in turn. Click on **Finish**.

Name of parameter	Data type	Contains information
Alert ID	String	Contains the SCOM Alert ID

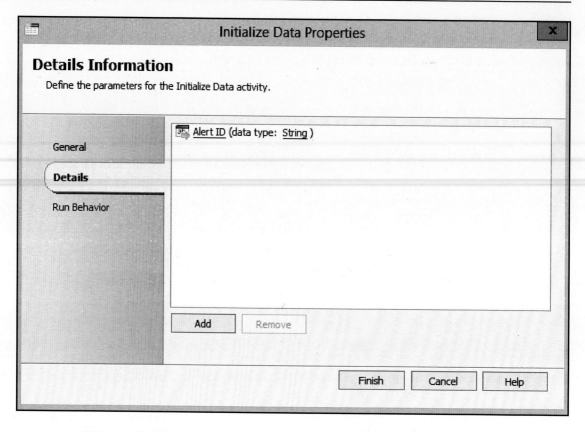

6. Click on **Finish**.
7. Navigate to the **Activities** section, click on **SC 2016 Operations Manager** and drag the **Get Alert** activity into the middle pane of the Runbook next to the **Initialize Data** activity:

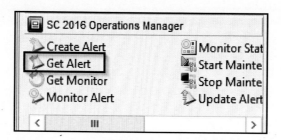

8. Link the **Get Alert** activity to the **Initialize Data** activity.
9. Double-click on the **Get Alert** activity and configure the connection to work with your System Center Operations Manager environment.

10. Configure the **Filter** like you see it in the screenshot:

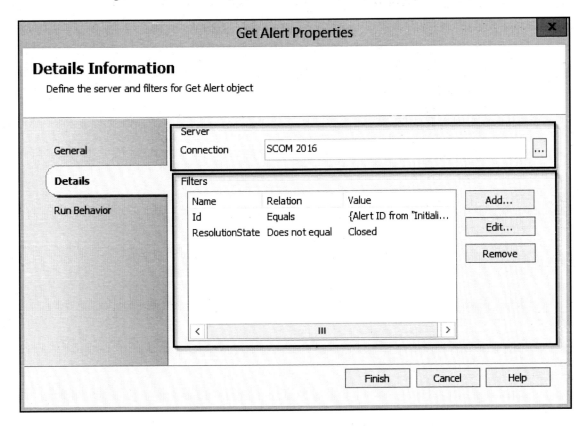

11. Navigate to the **Activities** section, click on **Utilities** and drag the **Query Database** activity into the middle pane of the Runbook next to the **Get Alert** activity:

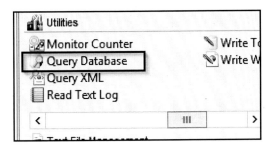

12. Link the **Query Database** activity to the **Get Alert** activity.
13. Double-click on the link between the **Query Database** activity and the **Get Alert** activity and configure the **Filter** like you see on the screenshot:

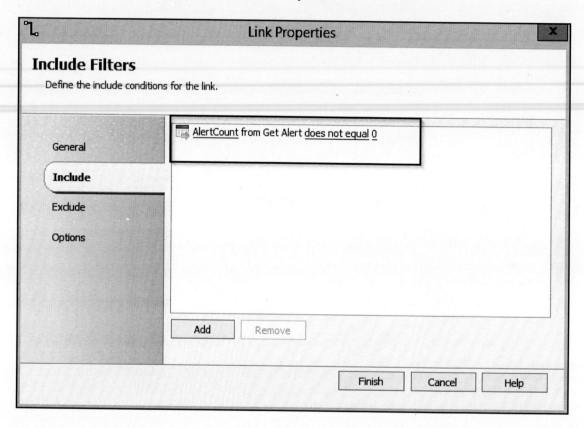

14. Rename the link to `count not equal 0` and change the color to orange.
15. Click **Finish**.

16. Double-click on the **Query Database** activity and configure the **Query** like you see in the screenshot:

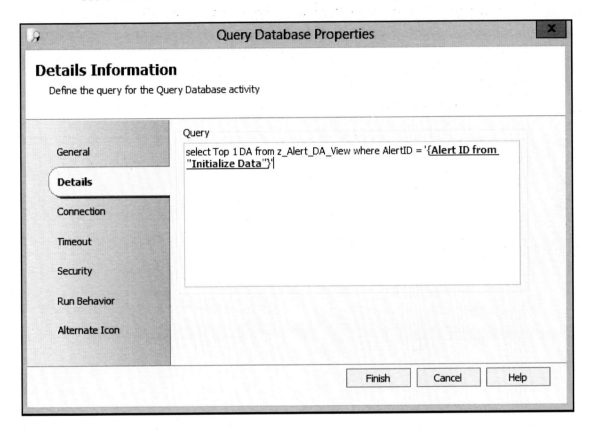

17. Switch to the **Connection** tab and configure like you see in the screenshot:

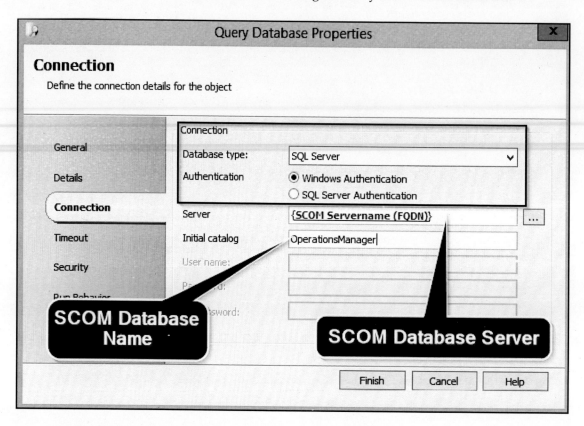

18. Click **Finish**.
19. Rename the **Query Database** activity to **Query for DA**.
20. Navigate to the **Activities** section, click on **Runbook Control** and drag the **Invoke Runbook** activity into the middle pane of the Runbook next to the **Query for DA** activity:

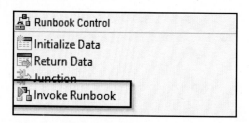

21. Link the **Query for DA** activity to the **Invoke Runbook** activity.
22. Rename the **Invoke Runbook** activity to **Update DA Alerts** to SCO
23. Double-click on the **Update DA Alerts to SCO** activity and select the **1.4.2.7-Update DA Alerts** Runbook and configure like on the screenshot:

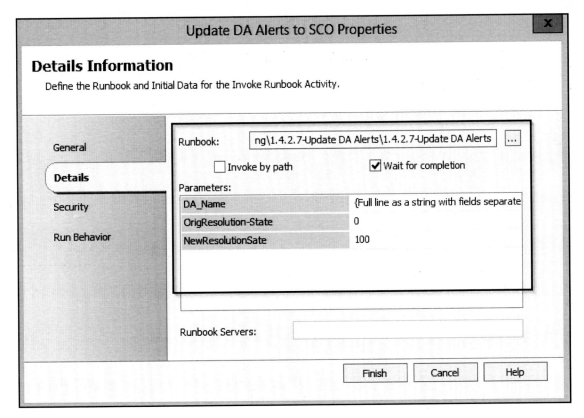

DA_Name	{Full line as a string with fields separated by ';' from "Query for DA"}
OrigResolutionState	0
NewResolutionState	100

24. Click **Finish**.

25. Navigate to the **Activities** section, click on **SC 2016 Operations Manager** and drag the **Get Alert** activity into the middle pane of the Runbook next to the **Update DA Alerts to SCO** activity:

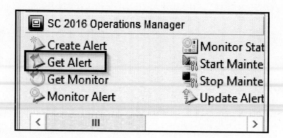

26. Link the **Get Alert** activity to the **Update DA Alerts to SCO** activity.
27. Double-click on the **Get Alert** activity and configure the connection to work with your System Center Operations Manager environment.
28. Configure the **Filter** like you see in the screenshot:

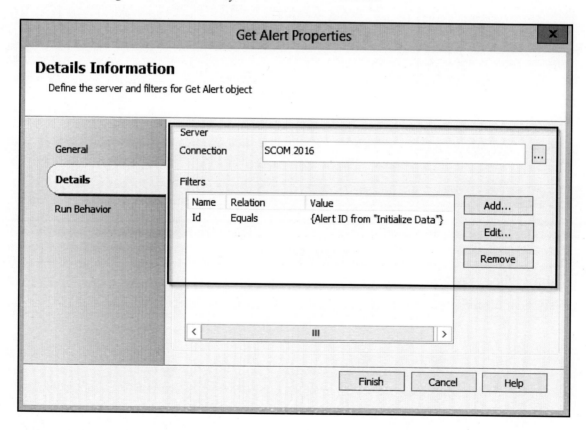

29. Navigate to the **Activities** section, click on **Runbook Control** and drag the **Invoke Runbook** activity into the middle pane of the Runbook next to the **Get Alert** activity:

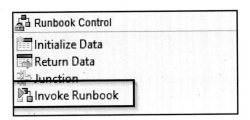

30. Rename the **Invoke Runbook** activity to **Notify Business Owner**.
31. Link the **Query for DA** activity to **Notify Business Owner** activity.
32. Double-click the **Notify Business Owner** activity and select the **1.4.2.3-Notify Business Owner** Runbook and Configure like the below table:

Alert Title	DA Alert: {Full line as a string with fields separated by ';' from "Query for DA"}
Business Service Name	{Full line as a string with fields separated by ';' from "Query for DA"}
Alert Description	\<b\>DA:\</b\> {Full line as a string with fields separated by ';' from "Query for DA"}\<br\> \<b\>Alert:\</b\> {Name from "Get Alert"}\<br\> \<b\>Source:\</b\> {MonitoringObjectDisplayName from "Get Alert"}\<br\> \<b\>Path:\</b\> {MonitoringObjectPath from "Get Alert"}\<br\> \<b\>Description:\</b\> {Description from "Get Alert"}\<br\> \<b\>Severity:\</b\> {Severity from "Get Alert"}\<br\> \<b\>Priority:\</b\> {Priority from "Get Alert"}\<br\>

33. Double-click the link between the **Get Alert** activity and the **Notify Business Owner** activity.

34. Configure the **Include** filter like in the screenshot:

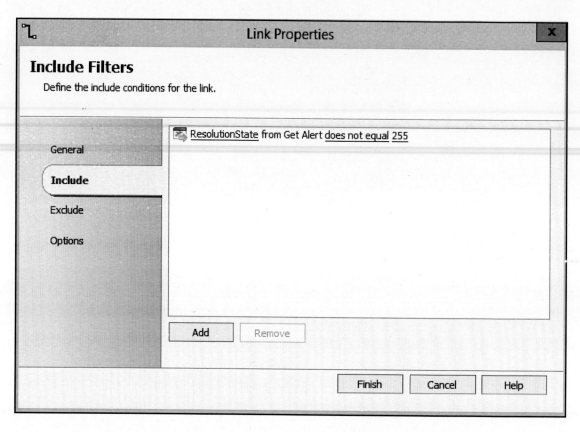

35. Rename it to No closed Alerts and change the color to orange.
36. Navigate to the **Activities** section, click on **Runbook Control** and drag the **Invoke Runbook** activity into the middle pane of the Runbook next to the **Get Alert** activity:

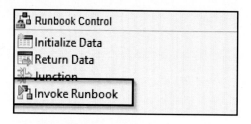

37. Rename the **Invoke Runbook** activity to **Notify Business Owner**.
38. Link the **Query for DA** activity to the **Notify Helpdesk** activity.
39. Double-click on the **Notify Helpdesk** activity and select the **1.4.2.4-Notify Helpdesk** Runbook and configure like this table:

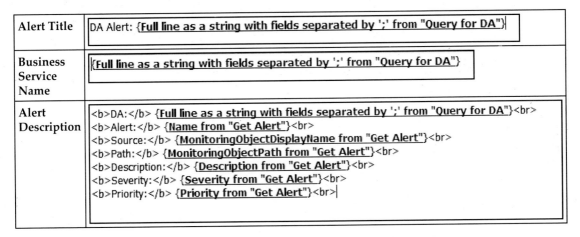

Alert Title	DA Alert: {**Full line as a string with fields separated by ';' from "Query for DA"**}
Business Service Name	{**Full line as a string with fields separated by ';' from "Query for DA"**}
Alert Description	\DA:\ {**Full line as a string with fields separated by ';' from "Query for DA"**}\ \Alert:\ {**Name from "Get Alert"**}\ \Source:\ {**MonitoringObjectDisplayName from "Get Alert"**}\ \Path:\ {**MonitoringObjectPath from "Get Alert"**}\ \Description:\ {**Description from "Get Alert"**}\ \Severity:\ {**Severity from "Get Alert"**}\ \Priority:\ {**Priority from "Get Alert"**}\

40. Navigate to the **Activities** section, click on **Runbook Control** and drag the **Invoke Runbook** activity into the middle pane of the Runbook next to the **Notify Helpdesk** activity:

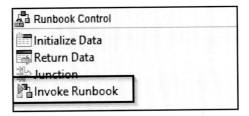

41. Link the **Notify Helpdesk** activity to the **Invoke Runbook** activity.
42. Rename the **Invoke Runbook** activity to **Update DA Alerts to Notified**.

43. Double-click on the **Update DA Alerts to** SCO activity and select the **1.4.2.7-Update DA Alerts** Runbook and configure like in the screenshot:

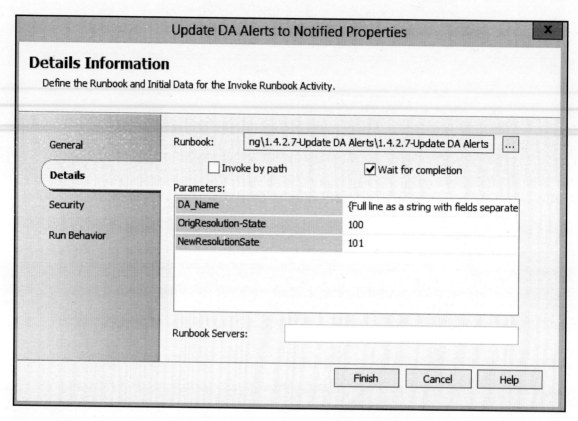

DA_Name	{Full line as a string with fields separated by ';' from "Query for DA"}
OrigResolutionState	100
NewResolutionState	101

44. Click **Finish**.

The Runbook should look like this:

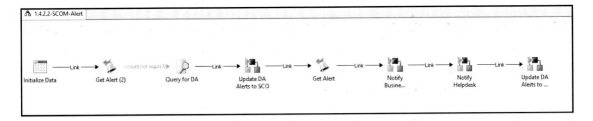

DA-Alert Runbook

This Runbooks will send a DA-Down Notification related to the SCOM Alert:

1. Navigate to the folder `1.4.2.1-DA-Alert`.
2. Right-click on the folder and then click on **New** and select **Runbook**.
3. Right-click the newly created Runbook and rename it to **1.4.2.1-DA-Alert**.
4. Navigate to the **Activities** section in the Runbook Designer. Click on **Runbook Control**, and select and drag an **Initialize Data** activity to the middle pane of the Runbook (start from the leftmost part of the pane and work towards the right as you add additional activities).
5. Right-click on **Initialize Data** | **Properties**. Click on **Add** and use the following table to configure the parameter in the **Details** section by clicking on each of the parameters in turn. Click on **Finish**.

Name of parameter	Data type	Contains information
Alert ID	String	Contains the SCOM Alert ID

6. Click on **Finish**.
7. Navigate to the **Activities** section, click on **SC 2016 Operations Manager** and drag a **Get Alert** activity into the middle pane of the Runbook next to the **Initialize Data** activity:

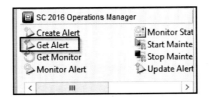

8. Link the **Get Alert** activity to the **Initialize Data** activity.
9. Double-click on the **Get Alert** activity and configure the connection to work with your System Center Operations Manager environment.
10. Configure the **Filter** like you see it in the screenshot:

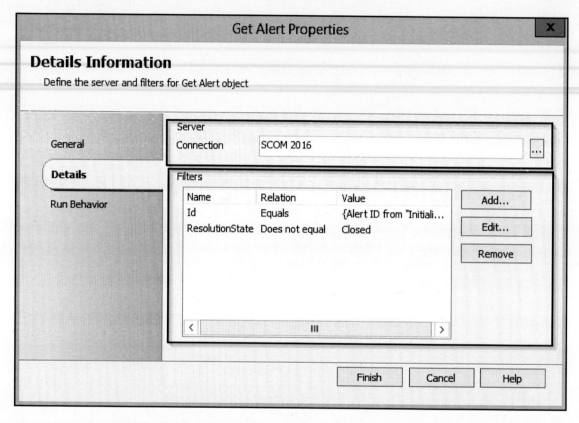

11. Navigate to the **Activities** section, click on **Utilities** and drag the **Query Database** activity into the middle pane of the Runbook next to the **Get Alert** activity:

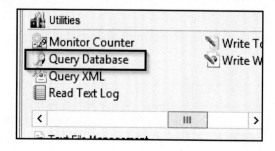

12. Link the **Query Database** activity to the **Get Alert** activity.

13. Double-click on the link between the **Query Database** activity and the **Get Alert** activity and configure the **Filter** like you see in the screenshot:

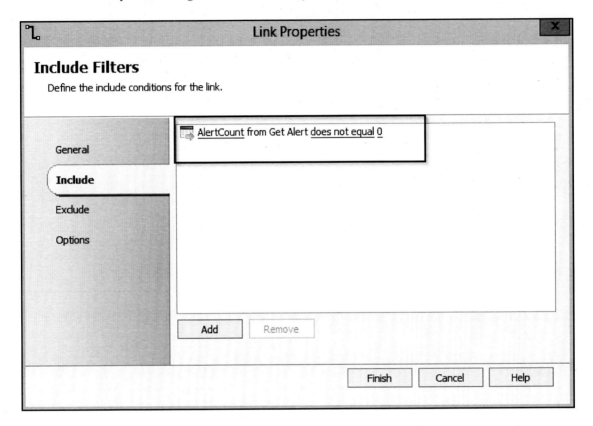

14. Rename the link to `count not equal 0` and change the color to orange.

15. Click **Finish**.

16. Double-click on the **Query Database** activity and configure the **Query** like you see in the screenshot:

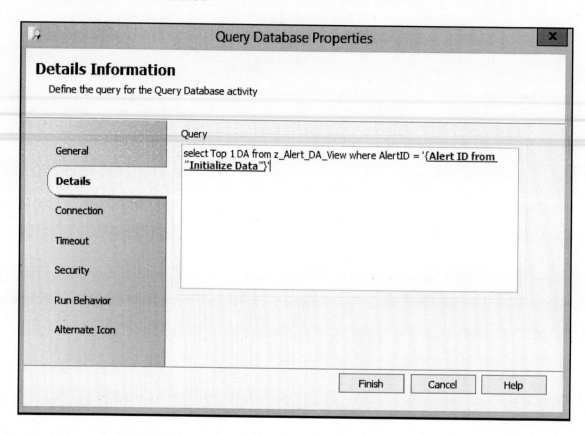

17. Switch to the **Connection** tab and configure like you see below:

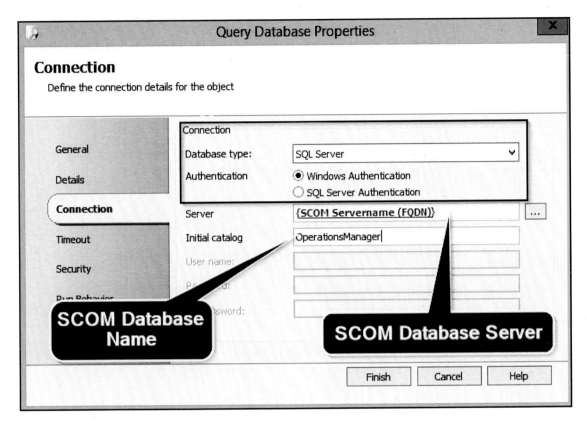

18. Click **Finish**.
19. Rename the **Query Database** activity to **Query for DA**.
20. Navigate to the **Activities** section, click on **Runbook Control** and drag the **Invoke Runbook** activity into the middle pane of the Runbook next to the **Query for DA** activity:

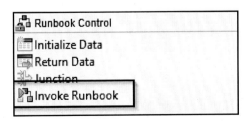

21. Link the **Query for DA** activity to the **Invoke Runbook** activity.
22. Rename the **Invoke Runbook** activity to Update DA Alerts to SCO.
23. Double-click on the **Update DA Alerts to SCO** activity and select the **1.4.2.7-Update DA Alerts** Runbook and configure like in the screenshot:

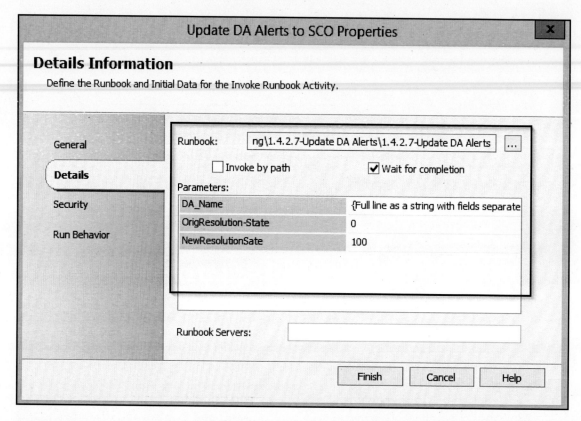

DA_Name	{Full line as a string with fields separated by ';' from "Query for DA"}
OrigResolutionState	0
NewResolutionState	100

24. Click Finish.

25. Navigate to the **Activities** section, click on **SC 2016 Operations Manager** and drag the **Get Alert** activity into the middle pane of the Runbook next to the **Update DA Alerts to SCO** activity:

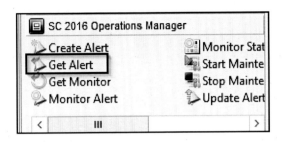

26. Link the **Get Alert** activity to the **Update DA Alerts to SCO** activity.
27. Double-click on the **Get Alert** activity and configure the connection to work with your System Center Operations Manager environment.
28. Configure the **Filter** like you see in the screenshot:

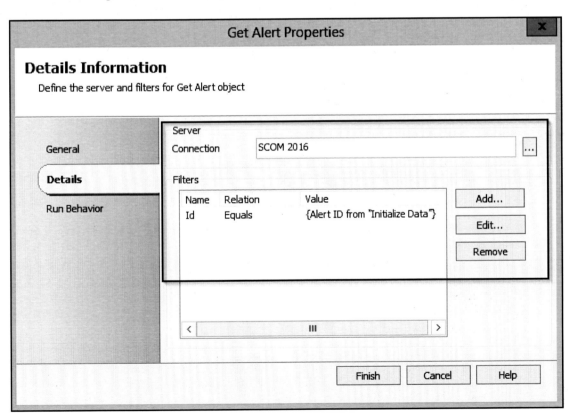

29. Navigate to the **Activities** section, click on **Runbook Control** and drag the **Invoke Runbook** activity into the middle pane of the Runbook next to the **Get Alert** activity.

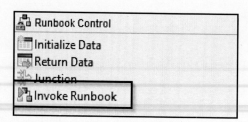

30. Rename the **Invoke Runbook** activity to **Notify Business Owner**.
31. Link the **Query for DA** activity to the **Notify Business Owner** activity.
32. Double-click on the **Notify Business Owner** activity and select the **1.4.2.3-Notify Business Owner** Runbook and configure like this table:

Alert Title	DA Alert: {**Full line as a string with fields separated by ';' from "Query for DA"**}
Business Service Name	{**Full line as a string with fields separated by ';' from "Query for DA"**}
Alert Description	\DA:\ {**Full line as a string with fields separated by ';' from "Query for DA"**}\ \Alert:\ {**Name from "Get Alert"**}\ \Source:\ {**MonitoringObjectDisplayName from "Get Alert"**}\ \Path:\ {**MonitoringObjectPath from "Get Alert"**}\ \Description:\ {**Description from "Get Alert"**}\ \Severity:\ {**Severity from "Get Alert"**}\ \Priority:\ {**Priority from "Get Alert"**}\

33. Double-click in the link between the **Get Alert** activity and the **Notify Business Owner** activity.
34. Configure the **Include** filter like on the screenshot:

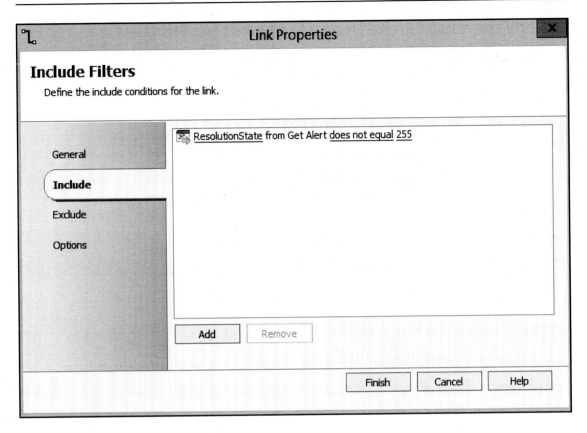

35. Rename the name to No closed Alerts and change the color to orange.
36. Navigate to the **Activities** section, click on **Runbook Control** and drag the **Invoke Runbook** activity into the middle pane of the Runbook next to the **Notify Business Owner** activity:

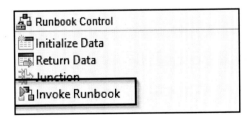

37. Rename the **Invoke Runbook** activity to **Notify Business Owner**.
38. Link the **Query for DA** activity to the **Notify external Helpline** activity.
39. Double-click on the **Notify external Helpline** activity and select the **1.4.2.5-Notify external Helpline** Runbook and configure like this table:

Alert Title	DA DOWN: {**Full line as a string with fields separated by ';' from "Query for DA"**}
Business Service Name	{**Full line as a string with fields separated by ';' from "Query for DA"**}
Alert Description	DA: {**Full line as a string with fields separated by ';' from "Query for DA"**} Alert: {**Name from "Get Alert"**} Source: {**MonitoringObjectDisplayName from "Get Alert"**} Path: {**MonitoringObjectPath from "Get Alert"**} Description: {**Description from "Get Alert"**} Severity: {**Severity from "Get Alert"**} Priority: {**Priority from "Get Alert"**}

40. Navigate to the **Activities** section, click on **Runbook Control** and drag the **Invoke Runbook** activity into the middle pane of the Runbook next to the **Notify external Helpline** activity:

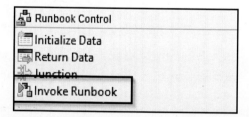

41. Link the **Notify external Helpline** activity to the **Invoke Runbook** activity.
42. Rename the **Invoke Runbook** activity to **Update DA Alerts to Notified**.

43. Double-click on the **Update DA Alerts to SCO** activity and select the **1.4.2.7-Update DA Alerts** Runbook and configure like in the screenshot:

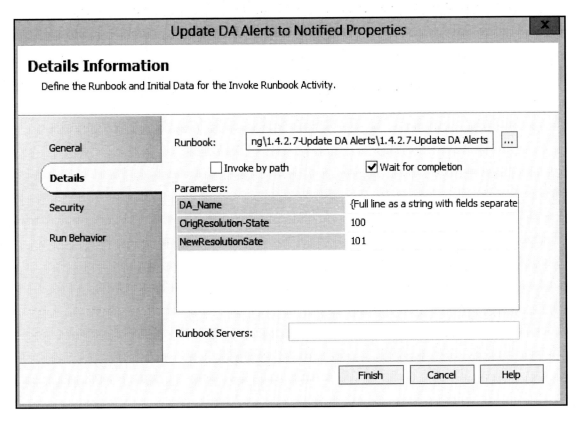

DA_Name	{Full line as a string with fields separated by ';' from "Query for DA"}
OrigResolutionState	100
NewResolutionState	101

44. Click **Finish**.

The Runbook should look like this:

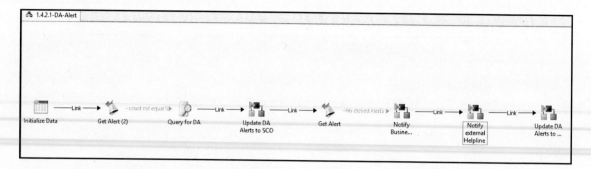

Monitoring Alerts Runbook

This Runbook is the important one, it will monitor your SCOM Alerts every 5 minutes and trigger the Alerting Runbooks build before:

1. Navigate to the folder **1.4.2-SCOM Alerting**.
2. Right-click on the folder and then click on **New** and select **Runbook**.
3. Right-click the newly created Runbook and rename it to **1.4.2-Monitor SCOM alert**.
4. Navigate to the **Activities** section in the Runbook Designer. Click on **Scheduling**, and select and drag the **Monitor Date/Time** activity to the middle pane of the Runbook (start from the leftmost part of the pane and work towards the right as you add additional activities).
5. Double-click the **Monitor Date/time** activity and configure like you see on the screenshot:

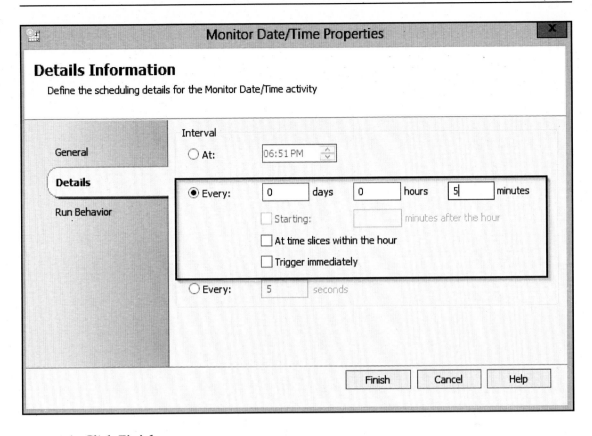

6. Click **Finish**.

7. Navigate to the **Activities** section, click on **Utilities** and drag the **Format Date/Time** activity into the middle pane of the Runbook next to the **Monitor Date/Time** activity:

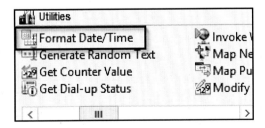

8. Link the **Monitor Date/Time** activity to the **Format Date/Time** activity.

9. Double-click on the **Format Date/Time** activity and configure the connection to work with your System Center Operations Manager environment:

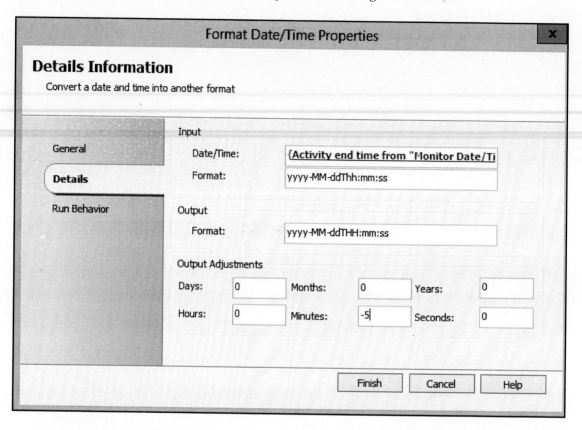

10. Navigate to the **Activities** section, click on **SC 2016 Operations Manager** and drag a **Get Alert** activity into the middle pane of the Runbook next to the **Format Date/Time** activity.

11. Link the **Format Date/Time** activity to the **Get Alert** activity.

12. Rename the **Get Alert** activity to **Get DA Alert**.

13. Double-click the **Get DA Alert** activity and configure the connection to work with your System Center Operations Manager environment.

14. Configure the **Filters** like in this table:

LastModified	Before	{Format Result from "Format Date/Time"}
ResolutionState	Equals	New
Name	Equals	Microsoft.SystemCenter.ServiceDesigner.GenericServiceHealth

15. Navigate to the **Activities** section, click on **Runbook Control** and drag the **Invoke Runbook** activity into the middle pane of the Runbook next to the **Get DA Alert** activity:

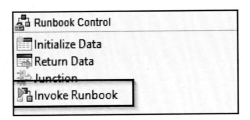

16. Rename the **Invoke Runbook** activity to **Notify DA Alert**.
17. Link the **Get DA Alert** activity to the **Notify DA Alert** activity.
18. Double-click on the **Notify DA Alert** activity and select the **1.4.2.1-DA Alert** Runbook and configure like in the screenshot:

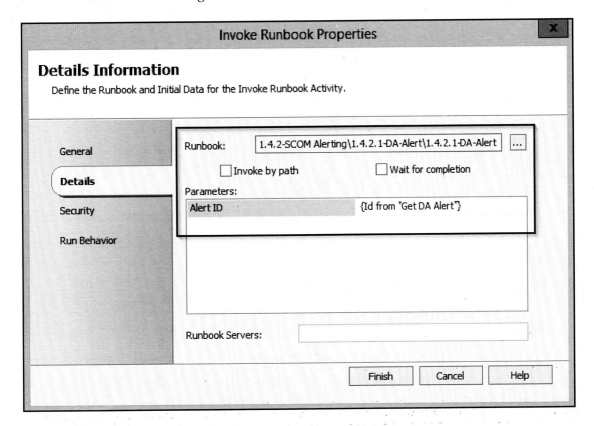

19. Click **Finish**.
20. Double-click the link between the **Get DA Alert** activity and the **Notify DA Alert** activity.
21. Configure the **Include** rule like in the screenshot:

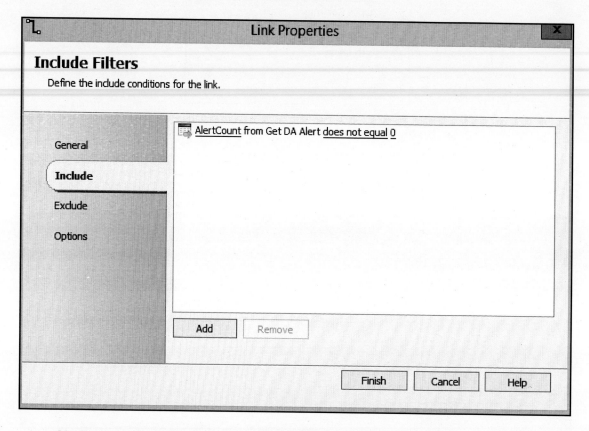

22. Rename the link to count != 0 and change the color to orange.
23. Click **Finish**.
24. Navigate to the **Activities** section, click on **Runbook Control** and drag the **Junction** activity into the middle pane of the Runbook next to the **Get DA Alert** activity:

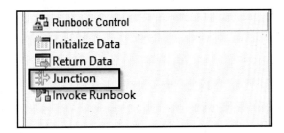

25. Link the **From at Date/Time** activity to the **Junction** activity.
26. Link the **Notify DA Alert** activity to the **Junction** activity.
27. Double-click the **Junction** activity and configure like in the screenshot:

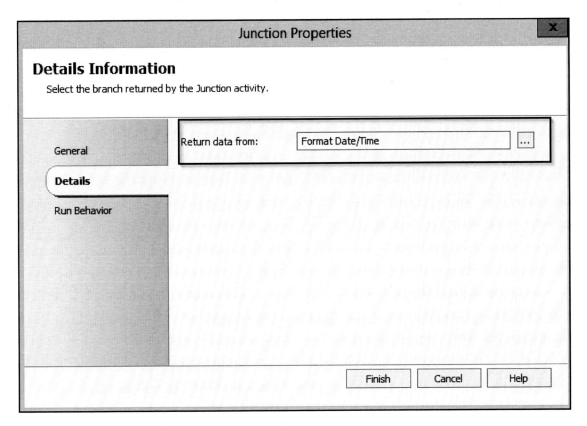

28. Navigate to the **Activities** section, click on **SC 2016 Operations Manager** and drag the **Get Alert** activity into the middle pane of the Runbook next to the **Junction** activity.

29. Link the **Junction** activity to the **Get Alert** activity.

30. Rename the **Get Alert** activity to `Get SCOM Alert`.

31. Double-click on the **Get SCOM Alert** activity and configure the connection to work with your System Center Operations Manager environment.

32. Configure the **Filters** like in this table:

LastModified	Before	{Format Result from "Format Date/Time"}
ResolutionState	Equals	New
Name	Does not Equal	Microsoft.SystemCenter.ServiceDesigner.GenericServiceHealth
Priority	Equals	High
Severity	Equals	Critical

33. Navigate to the **Activities** section, click on **Runbook Control** and drag the **Invoke Runbook** activity into the middle pane of the Runbook next to the **Get SCOM Alert** activity:

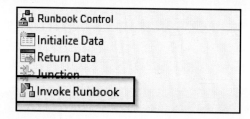

34. Rename the **Invoke Runbook** activity to **Notify SCOM Alert**.

35. Link the **Get SCOM Alert** activity to the **Notify SCOM Alert** activity.

36. Double-click on the **Notify SCOM Alert** activity and select the **1.4.2.2-SCOM Alert** Runbook and configure like in the screenshot:

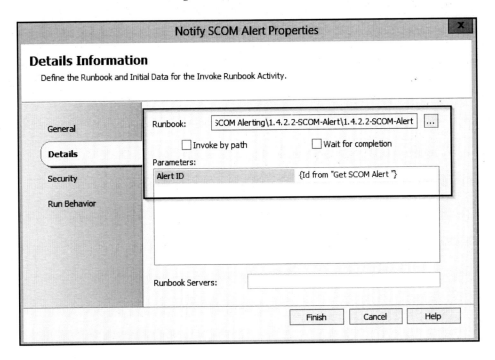

37. Click **Finish**.
38. Double-click the link between the **Get SCOM Alert** activity and the **Notify SCOM Alert** activity.

39. Configure the **Include** rule like in the screenshot:

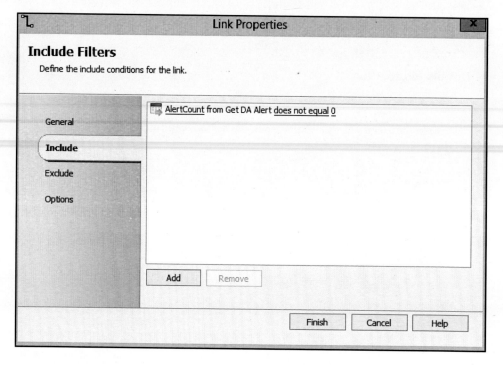

40. Rename the Link to count != 0 and change the color to orange.
41. Click **Finish**.

The Runbook should look like this:

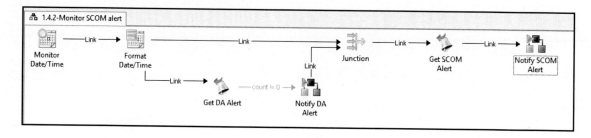

How it works...

You have to start the **1.4.2.Monitor SCOM Alert** Runbook.

This Runbook will check every 5 minutes if there are DA or SCOM alerts, older than 5 minutes. I recommend this, otherwise you can send false/positive alerts.

The difference between a DA Alert and a SCOM alert can be explained through a small example.

An example of a SCOM alert can be that, one server of a printer cluster is down, so the printers are still working, but care must be taken.

A DA Alert means, a complete DA is down, so both servers of your printer cluster are down, no one can print anymore, and we need to hurry up to solve this problem.

So we built two different Runbooks, so you can decide which to notify, depending on the priority of the alert.

There is more...

You can also extend your Notify Runbooks to send a SMS or make a phone call to your standby team, just add an additional Runbook to Send SMS, and call that new Runbook in your Master Alert Runbooks:

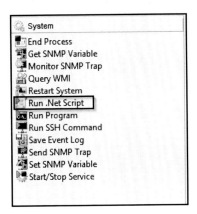

7
Doing More with Orchestrator

In this chapter, we will be providing recipes on how to do even more with System Center Orchestrator

- Starting an SCO Runbook using PowerShell
- Starting an SCO Runbook with the Orchestration Console
- Using SCOOSP to provide self service with SCO
- Maintaining and health checking SCO

Introduction

This last chapter will provide some advanced information to take your automation tasks to the next level and of course, how to take care of your Orchestrator environment.

Starting an SCO Runbook using PowerShell

Now we have built a lot of Runbooks, and hopefully brought up some fresh ideas of Runbooks that you would like to build, we are now at the point where we will learn how to trigger an SCO Runbook from outside and on how to get even more out of your Runbooks.

This recipe will show you how to use PowerShell to trigger a Runbook.

Getting ready

To complete this recipe, you need to build the Runbooks described in Chapter 4, *Building Advanced Runbooks*.

To test our PowerShell script, make sure you have PowerShell ISE installed on your server.

How to do it...

See how to use PowerShell and the SCO web service to start a Runbook, finish this Recipe to get a complete PowerShell Script:

1. Log on to your server or workstation and start PowerShell ISE

2. First, let's start by configuring our credentials. Enter the following:

```
#Credentials
$secpasswd = ConvertTo-SecureString "myhighsecurepassword" -
AsPlainText -Force
$mycreds   = New-Object
 System.Management.Automation.PSCredential ("doamin\user",
  $secpasswd)
```

3. Enter your password and user name to connect to your SCO Server.
4. Next, we need to configure our SCO server; enter the following:

```
#Orchestrator Server Name
$SCOServer = "svtgsco01"
```

5. Now let's configure our Runbook, we would like to call the input variable and parameter:

```
# Runbook to be called with a Property and Value
$RunbookName   = "1.2.2-Reboot a Server"
$RunbookInputProperty = "Servername (FQDN)"
$RunbookInputValue   = "svtgdc01"
```

6. Since the web service is working with the Runbook ID, let's get the ID with the following code:

```
# First get the GUID of the desired runbook
$OrchURI
 ="http://$($SCOServer):
 81/Orchestrator2012/Orchestrator.svc/Runbooks?`$filter=Name eq
 '$RunBookName'"
$ResponseObject=invoke-webrequest-Uri$OrchURI-methodGet-
 Credential$mycreds
$XML             = [xml] $ResponseObject.Content
$RunbookGUIDURL = $XML.feed.entry.id
```

7. Enter the following code to retrieve the XML content for the parameters:

```
$ResponseObject = invoke-webrequest -Uri
 "$($RunbookGUIDURL)/Parameters" -method Get -Credential
  $mycreds
   [System.Xml.XmlDocument] $XML = $ResponseObject.Content
```

8. Now enter the following code to create a function to obtain the input parameter:

```
function GetSCOProperty([System.Object]$XMLString,
[string]$Name, [string]$Direction, [string]$DesiredData){
   $nsmgr = New-Object
System.XML.XmlNamespaceManager($XMLString.NameTable)
$nsmgr.AddNamespace('d','http://schemas.microsoft.com/ado/2007/
 08/dataservices')
$nsmgr.AddNamespace('m','http://schemas.microsoft.com/ado/2007/
 08/dataservices/metadata')

   # Create an Array of Properties based on the 'Name' value

   $inputs = $XMLString.SelectNodes('//d:Name',$nsmgr)

   foreach ($parameter in $inputs){

      #Reset Property values
      $obName          =""
      $obId            =""
      $obType          =""
      $obDirection     =""
      $obDescription   =""

      $siblings = $($parameter.ParentNode.ChildNodes)
```

```
# Each of the sibling properties is identified
foreach ($elements in $siblings){
# write-host "Element = " $elements.ToString()
    If ($elements.ToString() -eq "Name"){
$obName = $elements.InnerText
    }
    If ($elements.ToString() -eq "Id"){
        $obId = $elements.InnerText
    }
    If ($elements.ToString() -eq "type"){
        $obType = $elements.InnerText
    }
    If ($elements.ToString() -eq "Direction"){
        $obDirection = $elements.InnerText
    }
    If ($elements.ToString() -eq "Description"){
        $obDescription = $elements.InnerText
    }
    If ($elements.ToString() -eq "Value"){
        # write-host "Value = "$elements.InnerText
        $obValue = $elements.InnerText
    }
}

    if (($Name -eq $obName) -and ($Direction -eq
    $obDirection)){
    # "Correct input found"
    #Return the Requested Property

    If ($DesiredData -eq "Id"){
        return $obId
    }
    If ($DesiredData -eq "Value"){
        return $obValue
    }
    }
    }
    return $Null
}
```

9. To use this function, and to get the Parameter ID, enter the following:

```
$RetreivedGUID = GetSCOProperty $XML
 $RunbookInputProperty "In" "Id"
```

10. Enter the next line to get the Runbook ID:

```
$urlstring = $RunbookGUIDURL
$RunbookID = $RunbookGUIDURL.Substring
  ($RunbookGUIDURL.Length - 38,36)
```

11. Before we can call the web service, we need to build the body to call the web service; enter the following:

```
$POSTBody = @"
<?xml version="1.0" encoding="utf-8" standalone="yes"?>
<entry xmlns:d="http://schemas.microsoft.com/ado/2007/
  08/dataservices"
  xmlns:m="http://schemas.microsoft.com/ado/2007/
  08/dataservices/metadata" xmlns="http://www.w3.org/2005/Atom">
<content type="application/xml">
<m:properties>
<d:RunbookId type="Edm.Guid">{$($RunbookID)}</d:RunbookId>
<d:Parameters>&lt;Data&gt;&lt;Parameter&gt;&lt;ID&gt;
{$($RetreivedGUID)}&lt;/ID&gt;&lt;Value&gt;
$($RunbookInputValue)&lt;/Value&gt;
  &lt;/Parameter&gt;&lt;/Data&gt;</d:Parameters>
</m:properties>
</content>
</entry>
"@
```

12. To start our Runbook, enter the following code:

```
# Submit Orchestrator Request
$OrchURI = "http://$($SCOServer):81/Orchestrator2012/
  Orchestrator.svc/Jobs/"
$ResponseObject = invoke-webrequest -Uri $OrchURI
-method POST -Credential $mycreds -Body
$POSTBody -ContentType "application/atom+xml"
```

How it works...

Let's try to execute the whole script. This is done by calling our **1.2.2-Reboot a Server** Runbook to reboot a server.

As we configured the Runbook name, the SCO web service will only work with the Runbook ID, so the script is first getting the Runbook ID and the Parameter ID to build the web request body from names we have provided.

In the end, we call the Runbook with the Runbook ID and Parameter ID to start the Runbook.

The Runbook Job, which will trigger the Runbook, will be created immediately but, sometimes it can take some time until the Runbook is triggered.

There is more...

If you start a Runbook, a Job will be created, and this Job is queued. It is therefore possible, that your Job will not be executed immediately. To enhance our script, see the following code snippets:

1. To get the Job ID, enter the following:

```
$XML               = [xml] $ResponseObject.Content
$RunbookJobURL     = $XML.entry.id
```

2. This code will wait until the Job is executed.

```
$status = $xml.entry.content.properties.Status
write-host "Current Status = " $status

do
{
    if($status -eq "Pending")
    {
        start-sleep -second 5
        $SleepCounter = $SleepCounter + 1
            if($SleepCounter -eq 20)
            {
                $DoExit="Yes"
            }
    }
    Else
    {
        $DoExit="Yes"
    }


    $ResponseObject=invoke-webrequest-Uri"
```

```
$($RunbookJobURL)"-methodGet-Credential$mycreds
    $XML        = [xml] $ResponseObject.Content
    $RunbookJobURL = $XML.entry.id
    $status = $xml.entry.content.properties.Status
    write-host "Current Status = " $status
}While($DoExit -ne "Yes")
```

Starting an SCO Runbook with the Orchestration Console

The Orchestration Console can be used to start a Runbook and enter the parameters. It will be installed with the first SCO Management Server.

Getting ready

On your server or workstation you would like to call the Orchestration Console, you need to install the Silverlight Plugin. The Orchestration Console uses Silverlight.

The URL to open the Orchestration Console should look like this: `http://svtgsco01:82/`.

There is an easy way to determine the URL:

1. Open the Orchestrator Runbook Designer.
2. Click on the **Orchestration Console** on the top navigation bar:

How to do it...

In this Recipe you will see how to use the Orchestration Console to start a Runbook:

1. Navigate to your Orchestration Console.

2. Navigate to your Runbook which you would like to start:

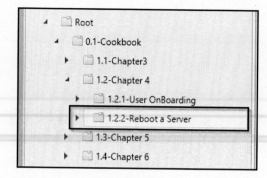

3. Now select the **Runbooks** tab in the center:

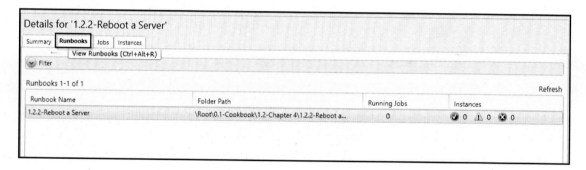

4. Select your Runbook and click on **Start Runbook**:

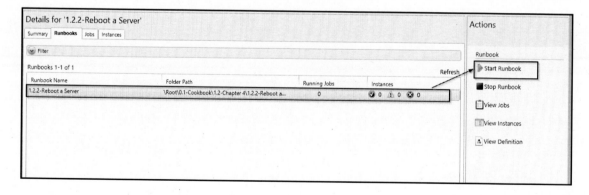

5. Enter the necessary parameters, and select a Runbook Server:

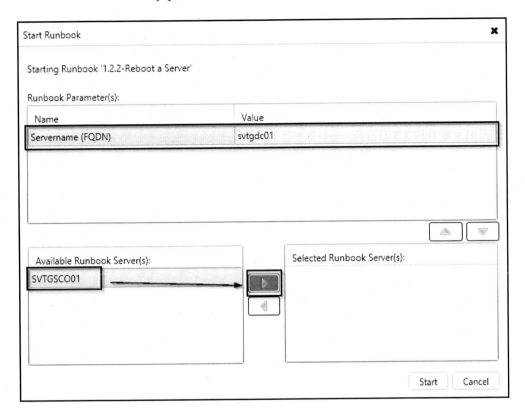

6. To start the Runbook, click on **Start**:

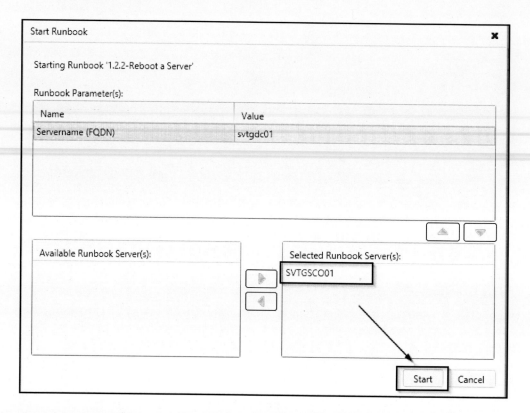

How it works...

The Runbook that you selected, will now be triggered. The Orchestration Console will also call the web service to trigger the Runbook. The web service will create a Job and the Job will be queued. When the Job is on top of the queue, the Runbook will be triggered.

There is more...

Switch to the **Jobs** tab to get more details about the Job and the time when the Runbook will be triggered:

You will also get the result of the Runbook, this means that you will know if the Runbook has been successful or if it threw an error.

Click on **View Instances** on the **Actions** bar at the right side, to see all instances of a special Runbook:

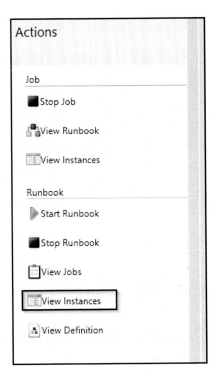

Using SCOOSP to provide self service with SCO

SCOOSP is the leading self service Portal for Automation in Microsoft Environment, where you can provide forms that will trigger a SCO Runbook, SMA Runbook, or Azure Automation Runbook.

This form can be used to provide self service for your IT staff and to your end users.

As we are writing a System Center Orchestrator Book, we will focus on SCO Runbooks to provide a self service form with SCOOSP.

In the end it doesn't matter, if you are using SCO, SMA, or Azure Automation.

SCOOSP is a third-party software, but free to try, feel free to download it from here: `http ://bit.ly/SCOOSP_Cookbook`.

Getting ready

To use SCOOSP, you need to download the trial version, see the *See also* section of *Using SCOOSP to provide self service with SCO* recipe for the download link.

Follow the support article to configure SCOOSP, navigate to the *See also* section of *Using SCOOSP to provide self service with SCO* recipe for details.

Make sure you can call the website URL and SCOOSP will be up and running.

How to do it...

SCOOSP is the leading self service Portal for Automation in Microsoft Environment, now lets see how easy it is to start a Runbook with SCOOSP:

1. Open your SCOOSP website as an admin and navigate to **Services**:

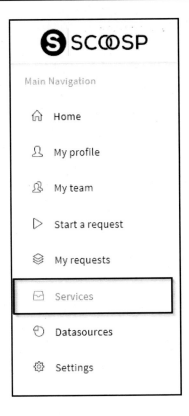

2. Click on **+New** to create a new service:

3. Enter all the details like you see in the screenshot:

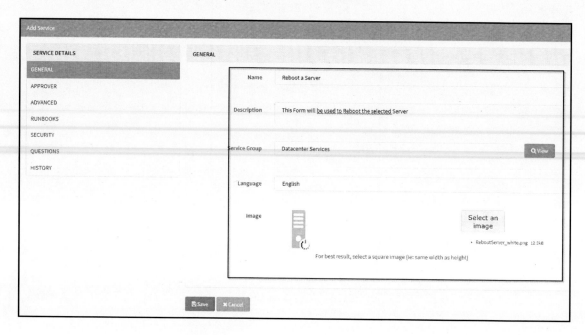

4. Switch to the **RUNBOOKS** tab:

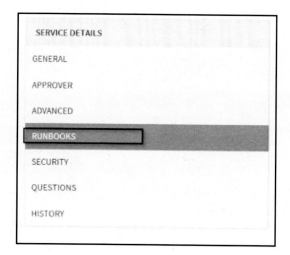

5. Select the **1.2.2-Reboot a Server** Runbook as the **Request New** Runbook:

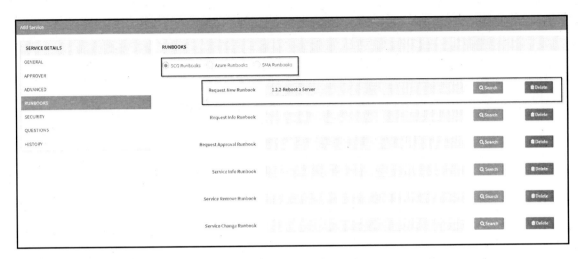

6. Next, select the **QUESTIONS** tab:

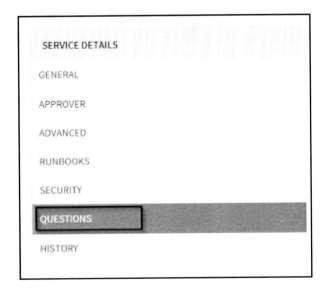

7. Here, select **LDAP Query** as the question type:

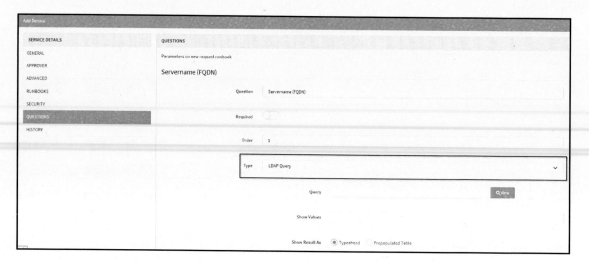

8. Enter the following LDAP Query in the **Query** field:

   (objectCategory=computer)

9. Also configure the value cn under **Show Values**:

Servername (FQDN)

Question	Servername (FQDN)
Required	
Order	1
Type	LDAP Query

Query	(objectCategory=computer) [Q View]
Show Values	cn

Show Result As — ◉ Typeahead ○ Prepopulated Table

Background Text

Visibility ◉ Always ○ Condition

10. Click on **Save**.

How it works...

An SCOOSP service is a form for providing different input parameters and questions, and to execute a Runbook. An SCOOSP service needs to be in a Service Group category. Both an SCOOSP Service and an SCOOSP Service Group can be limited to an Active Directory Group to provide a Role based Access Model.

As you have configured a service in SCOOSP, your users can use this service to help themselves by filling out the form and letting SCOOSP trigger the Runbook.

SCOOSP will provide the result of the Runbook to the user, and is also capable of displaying the return data from System Center Orchestrator Runbook.

SCOOSP is also using the web service of SCO and triggering the SCO Runbook.

There is more...

SCOOSP will provide a complete self service Portal where you can start a service for you and your team, manage your team, deploy SCCM software, and provide IT news as announcements or notes to your end users.

Start a service

To start a service in SCOOSP, navigate to the web page:

1. Click the **Start a request** page:

2. Select a user for whom the service should be started, we select **Myself**:

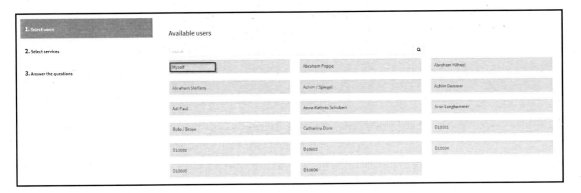

3. Click **Next**.
4. Now select the service you would like to start, select **Reboot a Server**:

5. Click **Next**.
6. Now type in your server, such as `svtgdc01`:

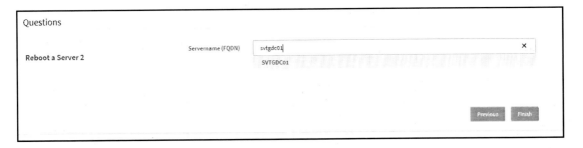

7. Click **Finish**.

8. Navigate to **My requests**:

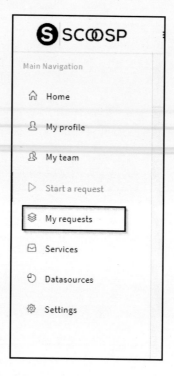

9. Navigate to the **History** tab.
10. Find your recently started service and click on the **i** button to get the Runbook Job result.

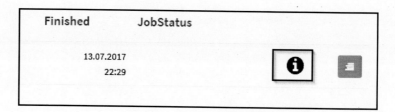

11. Click on the next symbol to get more information about this service:

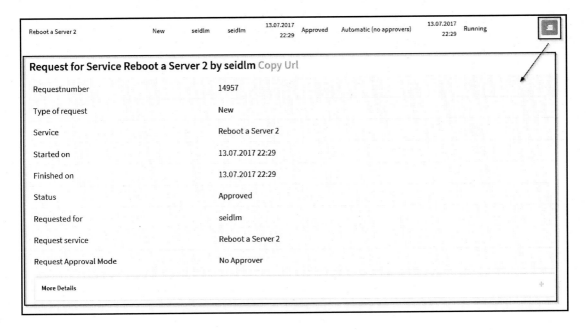

Manage you and your team

To manage you and your team, navigate to the SCOOSP web page:

1. Click on **My profile**:

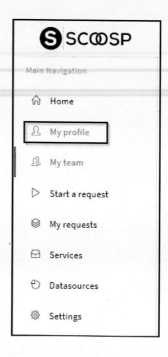

2. Now you will see some user details live from the Active Directory:

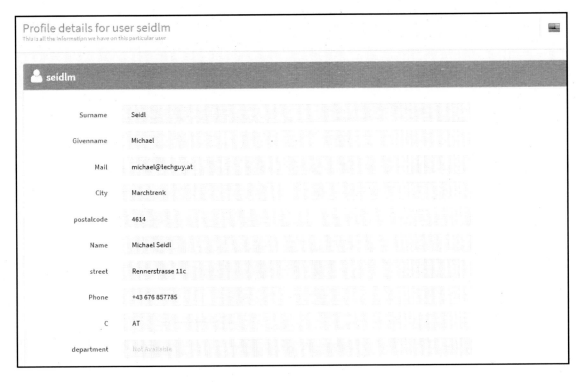

3. This information can be fully customized, with values that you would like to see.

4. Next, navigate to **My team**:

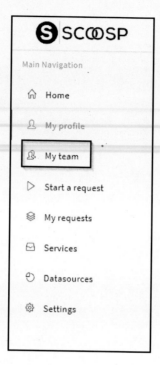

5. Now you will see all your team members related to the Managedby-Attribute or a Group Membership from Active Directory.

6. Click on the **View** button to see the user's details:

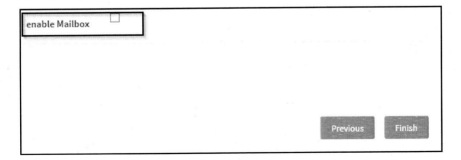

Abraham Poppe	Q View	Abraham Hähnel	Q View
Achim Demmer	Q View	Adi Paul	Q View
Boto / Brose	Q View	Catharina Dorn	Q View
D10003	Q View	D10004	Q View

Dynamic questions

SCOOSP also provides dynamic questions, for example:

You are providing an SCOOSP service for a user on-boarding, if someone is clicking the option **Enable Mailbox**, there will be an additional question on how much GB the user requires. This question is only available when a mailbox will be requested.

When **enable Mailbox** is False:

enable Mailbox

Previous   Finish

When **enable Mailbox** is True:

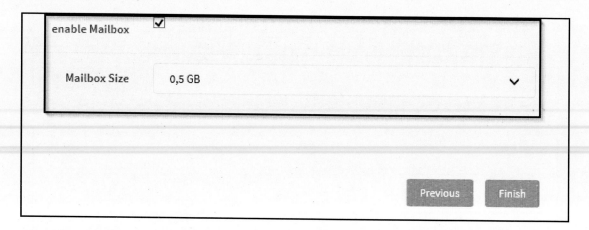

SCOOSP licensing

SCOOSP is free to test, however, if you decide to use SCOOSP, you will need to buy a license.

SCOOSP licensing is very easy, just count all your active, Active Directory users and see the detailed licensing at: `http://scoosp.com/pricing/` to determine your correct license.

Regardless of which license you choose, all features are included.

See also

- **SCOOSP**: Download trial version: `http://bit.ly/SCOOSP_Cookbook`
- **SCOOSP**: Configure SCOOSP: `https://support.scoosp.com/hc/en-us/sectio ns/201215402-First-Steps-with-SCOOSP`

Maintaining and health checking SCO

System Center 2016 Orchestrator will quickly become an important tool to automate your processes. So it will be necessary to keep SCO healthy.

Getting ready

One of the easiest ways to maintain SCO is a free community tool called Orchestrator Health Checker. The Orchestrator Health Checker will provide a small GUI to monitor your Runbook.

Download Orchestrator Health Checker from: `https://scorch.codeplex.com/releases/v iew/99063` and configure it as described in the link.

How to do it...

Follow the next steps to getting known of an awesome tool to health check your SCO Environment:

1. Navigate to the install directory and open `Orchestrator Health Checker.exe`:

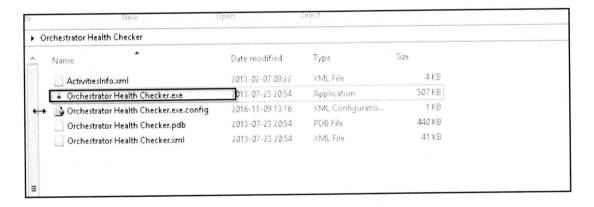

2. See the screenshot for an overview:

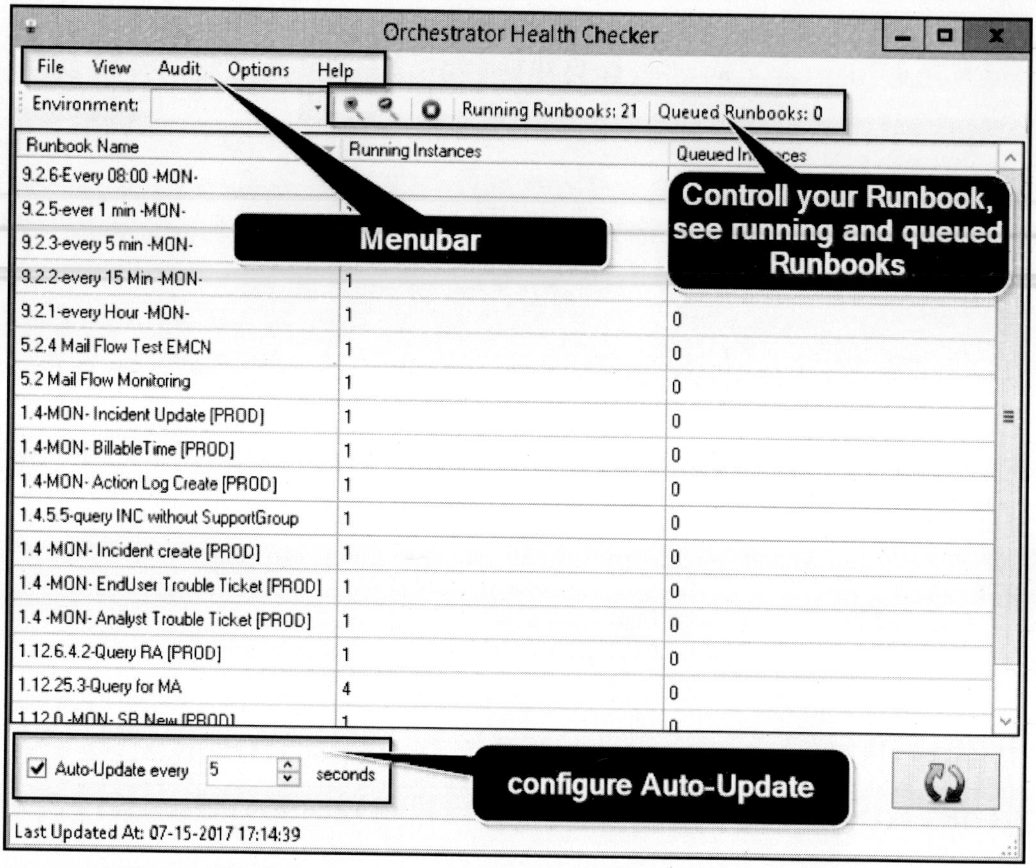

How it works...

Orchestrator Health Checker uses the SQL Database to gather all the information and uses the web service to stop or start a Runbook.

There is more...

Orchestrator Health Checker provides a lot of useful information and options.

1. Navigate to the installation directory and open `Orchestrator Health Checker.exe`:

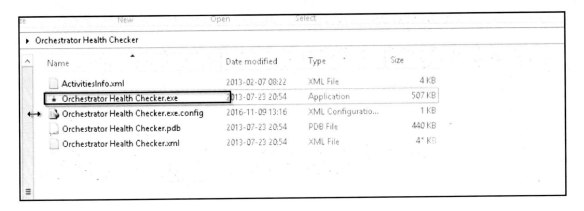

2. Navigate to **Options** and select **System Health** to get an overview of your environment:

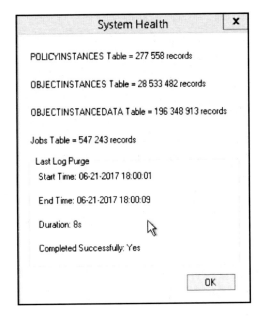

3. Click **OK** to close that window.

Click through the menu to see all of the features Orchestrator Health Check provides.

See also

Orchestrator Health Check – Documentation: `https://scorch.codeplex.com/documentat ion`

Index